Contents

Chapter 1 – Excel Basics	2
Chapter 2 – Calculations	11
Chapter 3 – Documenting a Project	19
Chapter 4 – Modelling	25
Chapter 5 – Formatting	36
Chapter 6 – Naming and Sorting Ranges	42
Chapter 7 – Validation and VLookup	49
Chapter 8 – Macros and Buttons	58
Chapter 9 – Charts	71
Index	80

Chapter 1

Excel Basics

Getting started

If you are starting this book, you already know what an Excel workbook looks like, and how to enter labels, numbers and formulae. If you are a little rusty, this chapter will soon bring you up to speed again.

Load Microsoft Excel.

You will see the following screen:

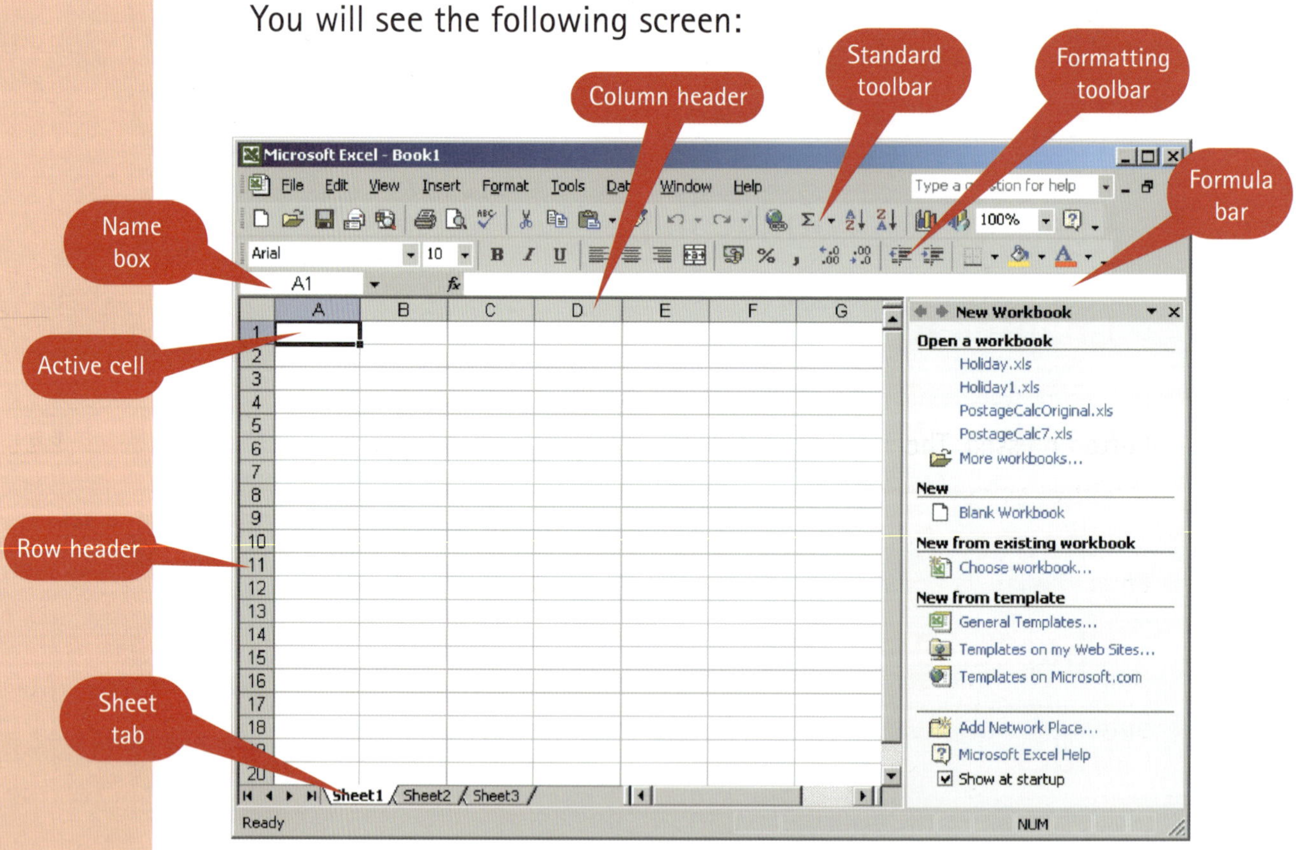

Figure 1.1: The opening screen

Click the "X" in the top right corner of the Task Pane to hide it or right-click any other button on the toolbar and deselect Task Pane.

Project: Prepare a holiday budget

You are going to enter details of a driving holiday to France in order to work out the total costs. First of all you need to think what the main expenses will be. There will be the cost of getting across the Channel, the cost of petrol to reach your destination, accommodation in a hotel or maybe a campsite, food, entertainment, unexpected emergencies such as car breakdown and so on.

In this exercise we will just calculate three main costs to illustrate the use of a spreadsheet. These are:

Petrol

Accommodation

Food

- Starting in cell A1, type the title European Holiday Planner and press Enter or the Tab key to move to another cell.

- Highlight cells A1 to F1 by dragging across them with the left mouse button pressed. Then click the Merge and Center button to centre the titles across columns A to F.

- Enter the labels Petrol, Accommodation and Food in cells A4 to A6.
- Double-click the border between the column headers A and B to automatically set column A to the right width.

	A	B	C	D	E	F
1			European Holiday Planner			
2						
3						
4	Petrol					
5	Accommodation					
6	Food					
7						

Figure 1.2: Starting the spreadsheet

Saving your spreadsheet

It's a good idea to save your work early on, and every few minutes as you work.

- Save the workbook as **Holiday** in your chosen folder. Excel will automatically add the extension **.xls**.

Moving and deleting cell contents

Suppose you have accidentally entered these labels in the wrong cells. You can move them easily.

- Highlight cells A4 to A6.
- Place the pointer over the bottom border round the three cells. It will change to an upward-pointing, diagonal arrow.
- Hold down the left mouse button and drag down one cell. The labels now appear in A5 to A7.
- Maybe you want to delete the cell contents and start again. With the cells still highlighted, press the **Delete** key. The cell contents disappear.

- Now press the **Undo** button twice to undo the last two actions. Your labels should reappear in cells A4 to A6.
- Enter the labels and numbers as shown in Figure 1.3. To get the Euro symbol, press **Alt Gr** (to the right of the Space Bar) and **4** (on the main keypad, not the numeric keypad) together.
- Adjust column widths by dragging across column headers B to F and double-clicking the border between any two column headers.

Tip:

You can also select **Insert, Symbol** from the Menu Bar to insert the Euro symbol. Select Font **(normal text)** and subset **Currency Symbols.**

	A	B	C	D	E	F
1	European Holiday Planner					
2						
3		Quantity	Unit	Unit Cost (€)	Total (€)	Total (£ Sterling)
4	Petrol	300	Miles			
5	Accommodation	4	Nights			
6	Food	12	Meals			
7						
8	Total Cost					

Figure 1.3

Entering unit costs

You can enter estimates for the unit costs of each item. Later we will calculate more accurately the unit cost of petrol needed for travelling one mile.

The unit costs will be entered in Euros (€). We will assume for now that it costs about 1 Euro to travel ten miles. (There are usually about 1.5 Euros to the pound, though this varies from year to year. You can find out the current rate from the newspaper or the Internet.)

- Enter unit costs of 0.1, 50 and 10 for Petrol, Accommodation and Food in D4 to D6.

Entering and copying formulae

In cell E4, you need to enter the formula =B4*D4. You can enter the formula by typing it in or by 'pointing', as described below:

- In cell E4, type =.
- Click in cell B4 and then type *.
- Click in cell D4. Notice that the formula you need has appeared in cell E4.
- Press Enter to complete the formula. The number 30 appears in E4.

Tip:
You can type cell references using either upper- or lower-case letters.

Tip:
For now, ignore the Autofill Options button.

- With E4 selected, click and drag the little square (the **Fill handle**) at the bottom right-hand corner of the cell to cells E5 and E6. This copies the formulae.
- Click in cell E5. What formula is shown in the Formula Bar?
- Click in cell E6. What formula is shown in the Formula Bar?

Tip:
The formula in E6 is =B6*D6.

Absolute and relative referencing

By default, Excel uses **relative referencing** in formulae. So for example, Excel interprets the formula in cell E4 as "Multiply the cell three places to the left by the cell one place to the left". When you copy the formula to cell E5, you are copying these instructions, and the formula, relative to where it is entered, becomes **=B5*D5**.

Sometimes you don't want the cell reference to change when you copy a formula. You then need to use an **absolute reference**. Here is an example.

- In cell A14, type **Exchange Rate (€ to the £)**. Press Enter. Widen the cell to hold the text without overflowing.
- In cell B14, type **1.5**. (Assume there are 1.5 Euros to the £.)
- In cell F4, type the formula **=E4/$B$14**. The $ signs tells Excel that when you copy the formula to other cells, **B** is to stay as **B** and **14** is to stay as **14**.
- Copy the formula to cells F5 and F6 by dragging the Fill handle.

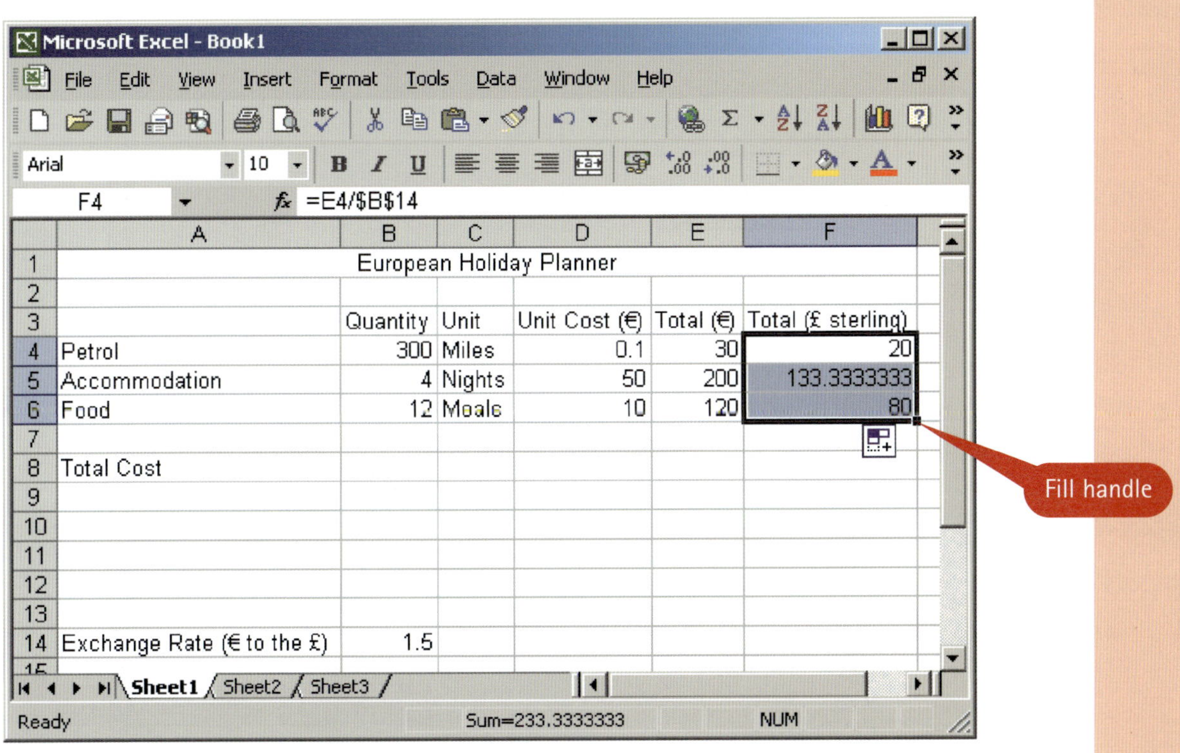

Figure 1.4

- Click in cell F5 and look at the formula in the Formula bar. You will see that the formula contains the absolute reference **$B$14**.

What would happen if you had used a relative, rather than absolute, reference to cell B14? Try it and find out!

Formatting numbers

Cells in columns D and E need to be formatted as Euros.

- Drag across cells D4 to E10 to select these cells.
- From the menu bar select Format, Cells...
- Choose Currency from the Category menu and € Euro (€123) from the Symbol menu.
- Click OK.

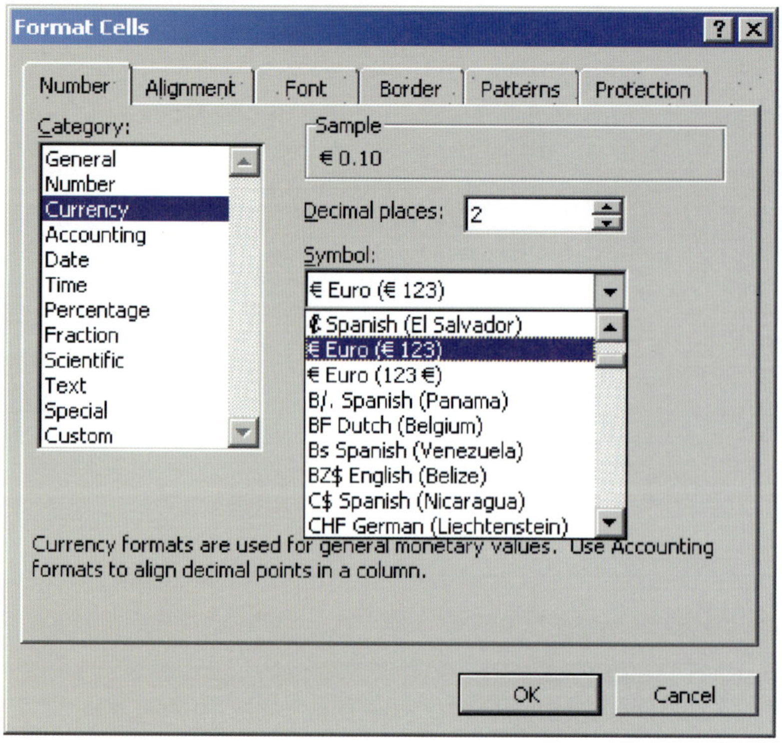

Figure 1.5: Formatting cells in foreign currency

- Select cells F4 to F10. You can format these cells as English currency in the same way, or you can use a shortcut, as follows:

- Click the **Currency** button on the Formatting toolbar.

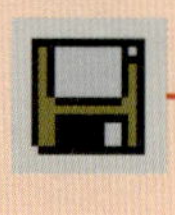

- Save your workbook by clicking the **Save** button on the Standard toolbar.

Formatting text

First of all you can make the title and all the column and row headings bold.

- Select cells A1 to F3. Then hold down the **Ctrl** key while you select A4 to A8 and A14. Press the **Bold** button on the Formatting toolbar.

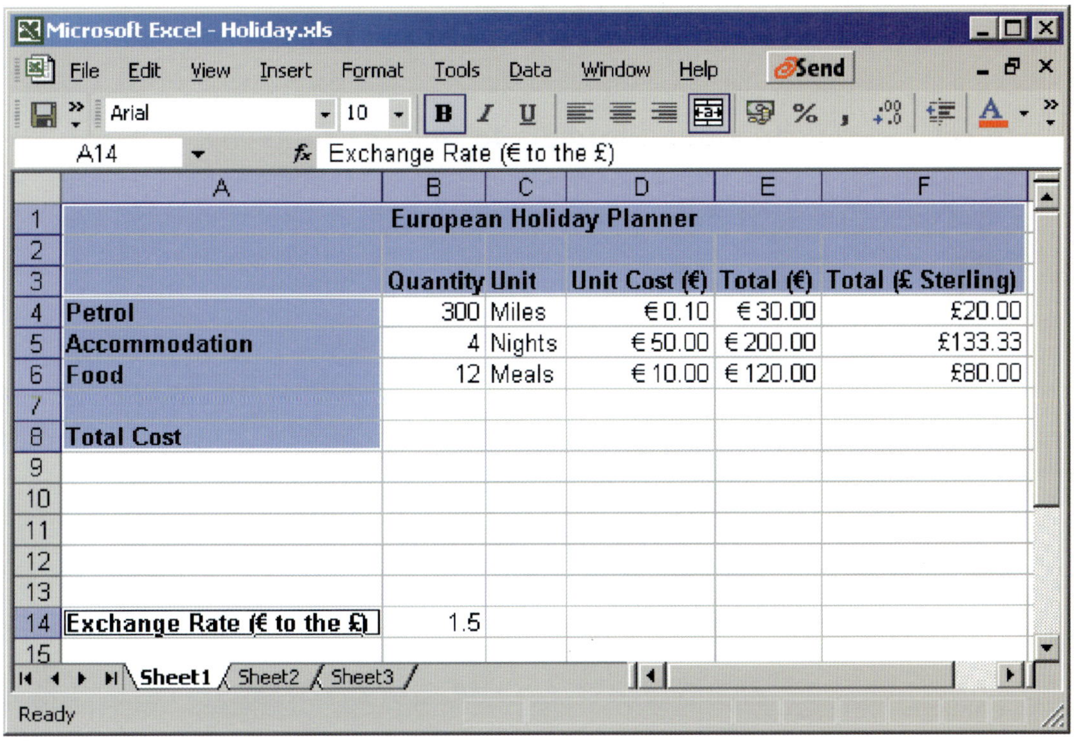

Figure 1.6: Selecting non-adjacent cells for formatting

- Adjust column widths to accommodate the bold text.

Now you can make the title more striking.

- Select cell A1, which contains the title, and increase the font size to 20.

- Choose a Fill colour of Lime Green.

Entering a SUM formula

In cell F8 you can enter a formula to find the total cost of the holiday.

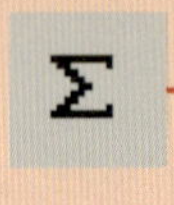

- Click in cell F8 and then click the **AutoSum** button.
- Excel guesses that you want to sum F4 through F7. This is correct, so press **Enter**.

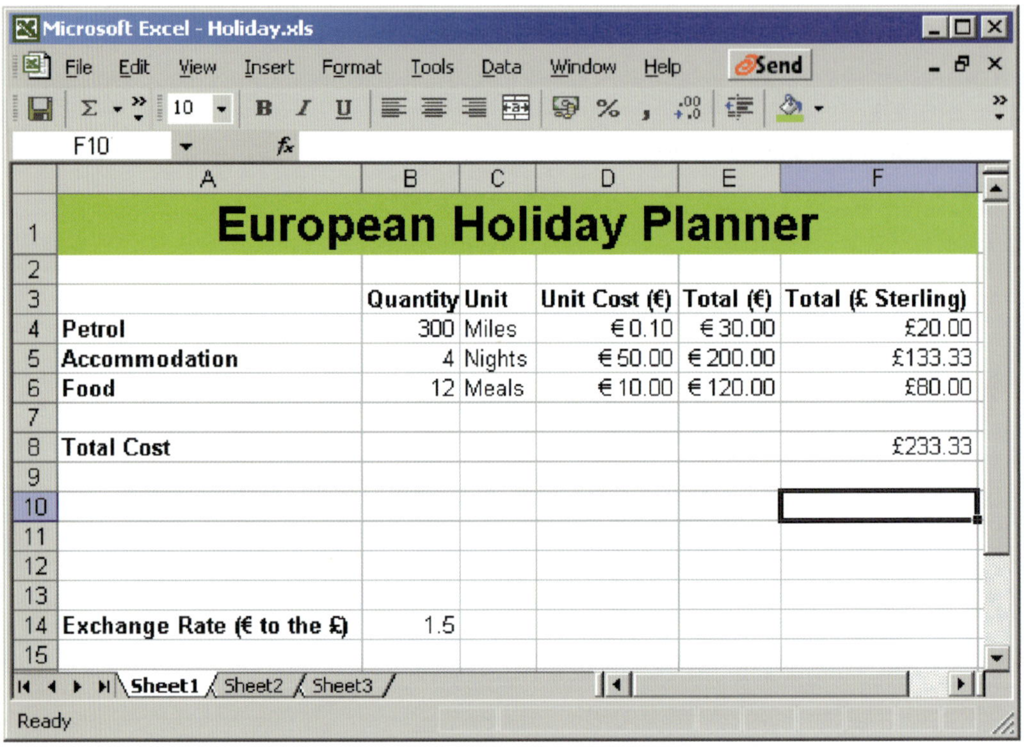

	A	B	C	D	E	F
1	European Holiday Planner					
2						
3		Quantity	Unit	Unit Cost (€)	Total (€)	Total (£ Sterling)
4	Petrol	300	Miles	€ 0.10	€ 30.00	£20.00
5	Accommodation	4	Nights	€ 50.00	€ 200.00	£133.33
6	Food	12	Meals	€ 10.00	€ 120.00	£80.00
7						
8	Total Cost					£233.33
9						
10						
11						
12						
13						
14	Exchange Rate (€ to the £)	1.5				
15						

Figure 1.7

- Save and close your worksheet.

Chapter 2

Calculations

In this chapter you will be doing some more work on the Holiday workbook started in Chapter 1.

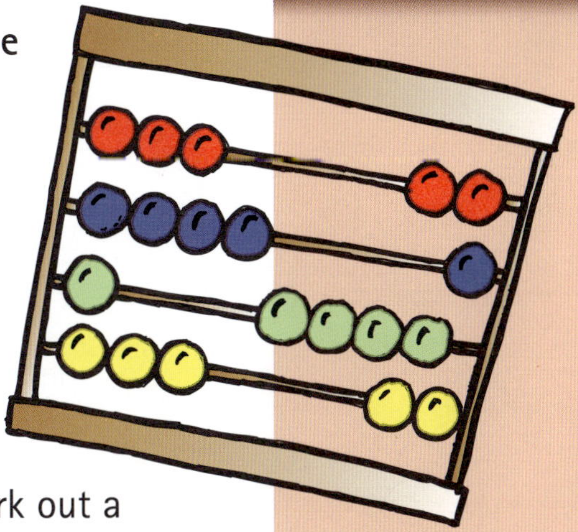

Load Excel and open the workbook Holiday.xls.

You are going to work out the cost in Euros per mile of travel. This will depend on the number of miles to the gallon that your car does, and the cost of petrol. The number of miles to the gallon will depend on whether you use motorways or other roads, so we will work out a unit cost for both possibilities.

Preparing a conversion table

First of all you need to prepare a table to work out the unit cost. Since petrol is sold in litres but mileage is often given in miles to the gallon, you need to know how many litres there are in a gallon. You also need to know the cost of a litre of petrol. These figures are given in Figure 2.1.

Enter the labels and figures as shown in Figure 2.1.

Make all the labels bold.

Tip:

For more buttons, click the **Toolbar Options** button.

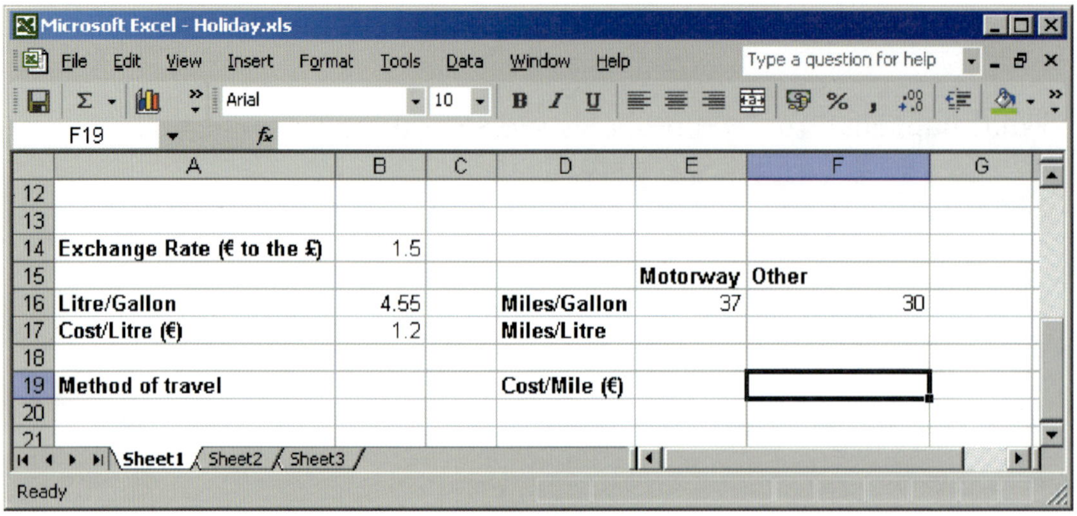

Figure 2.1

Cost per litre should be shown to 2 decimal places.

- Click in cell B17.
- Press the **Increase Decimal** button.

The headings **Motorway** and **Other** would look better right-justified.

- Select cells E15 and F15 containing these two headings.
- Press the **Align Right** button.

Calculating miles/litre

This requires Maths skills! Work it out roughly first. If the car does 37 mpg, and a gallon is about 4 litres, the car will only do about a quarter as many miles to the litre. You need to divide the Miles/Gallon by the Litres/Gallon.

- In cell E17 enter the formula **=E16/B16**.
- Select cells E17 and F17 and from the menu select **Format**, **Cells**.
- Format the cells as **Number**, **2** decimal places.

Copy cell E17 to cell F17 by dragging the Fill handle.

What happens? You will probably see something like Figure 2.2.

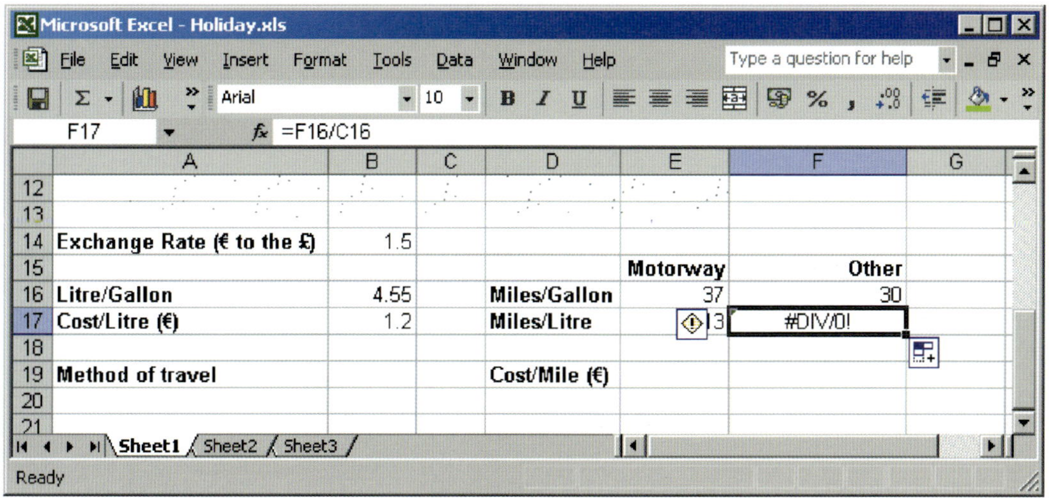

Figure 2.2

Absolute cell references

The formula in the cell is **=F16/C16**, but we want **=F16/B16**. We should have made B16 an **absolute** reference, not a **relative** reference.

An absolute reference is one that does not change when you move or copy it to a different cell.

- Click in cell E17.
- In the Formula Bar, edit the formula so that it says **=E16/$B$16**.
- Copy the formula to cell F17.

Now you need to calculate the cost per mile in Euros (€).

If the car does 8.13 miles to the litre, it uses 1 divided by 8.13 litres for one mile.

1 litre costs 1.2 €

So 1/8.13 litres cost 1.2/8.13 €. That is the unit cost per mile.

Tip:

You can see how the error happened by clicking the **Error** button, and selecting **Show Calculation Steps...**

Tip:
Try typing **=B17**, then press Function Key F4. This puts in the $ signs automatically!

- In cell E19, type the formula **=$B$17/E17**.
- Copy the formula to cell F19.
- Format these two cells as Euros, to 2 dp.

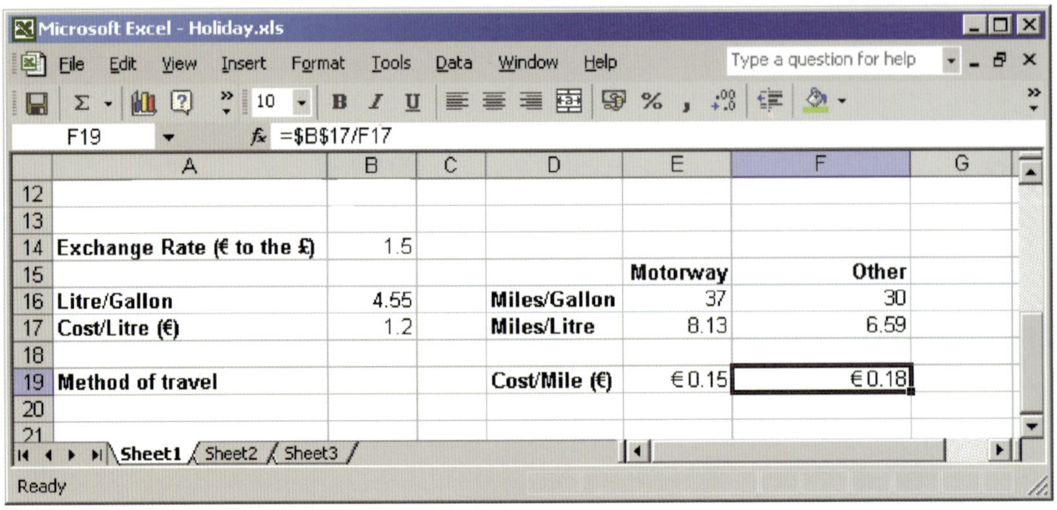

Figure 2.3

The IF function

The unit cost per mile can now be put in cell D4 in the top part of the worksheet. However, the unit cost will depend on the method of travel. We can put a formula in the cell that will give a different answer depending on the method of travel entered in cell B19.

- In cell B19 enter M for Motorway.
- Delete the current contents of cell D4 by selecting it and pressing the Delete key.
- Still in cell D4, press the down arrow by the AutoSum button.
- In the Paste Function window, select Logical in the left hand list, and IF in the right hand list.
- Select More Functions....
- In the Insert Function window, select Logical in the category list and IF in the function list.

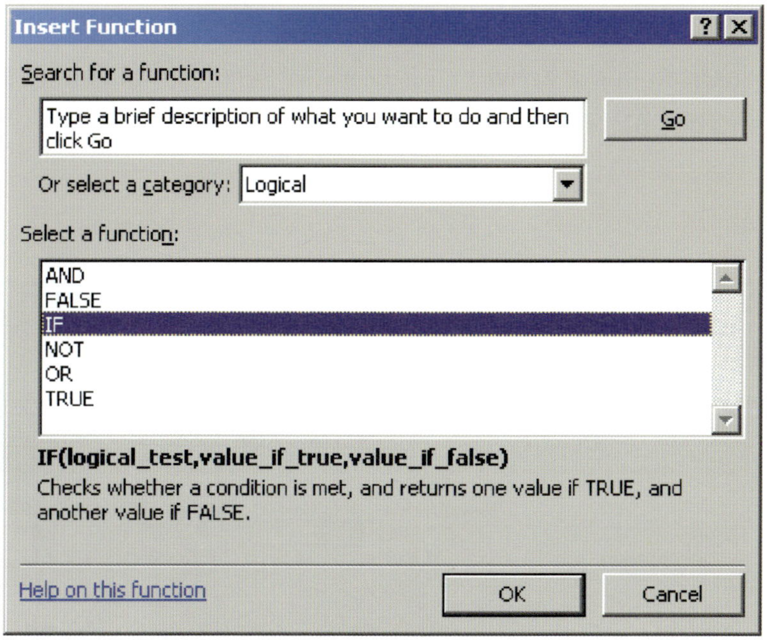

Figure 2.4: Selecting a function

- Click **OK**.
- In the next window, with the cursor in the **Logical_test** box, click in cell B19. Complete the entry by typing **="M"**.
- Tab to the second box, **Value_if_true**. Click in cell E19.
- Tab to the next box, **Value_if_false**. Click in cell F19.

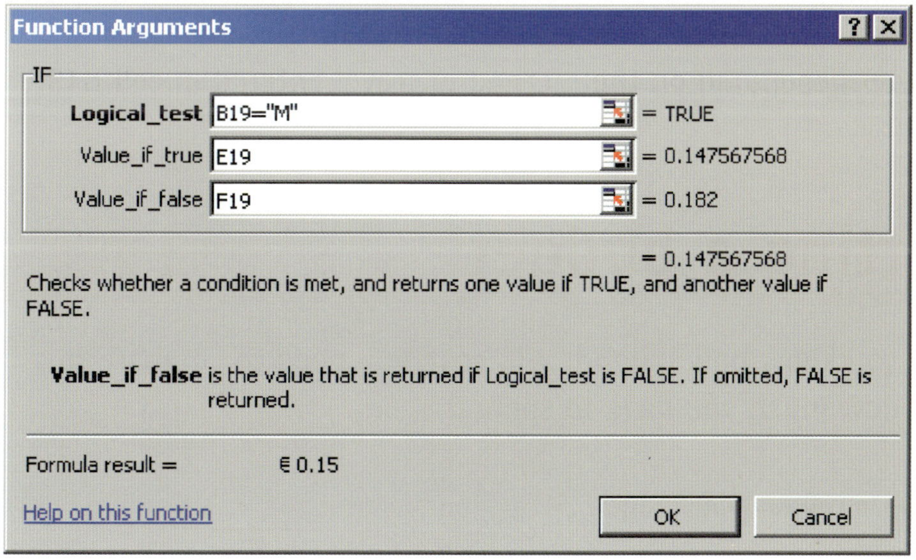

Figure 2.5

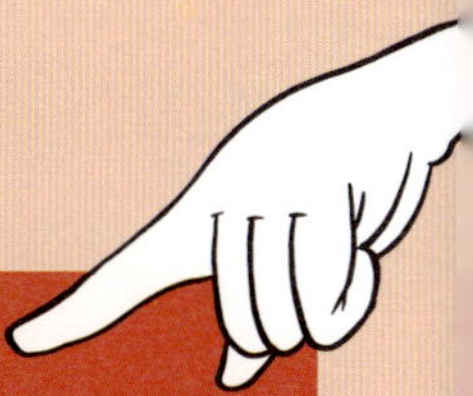

Tip:

You can drag the **Paste Function** dialogue box out of the way!

Read the text in this window. It tells you that the value in E19 will be inserted in the active cell if B19="M", and the value in F19 will be inserted if B19 is not equal to "M".

Click OK.

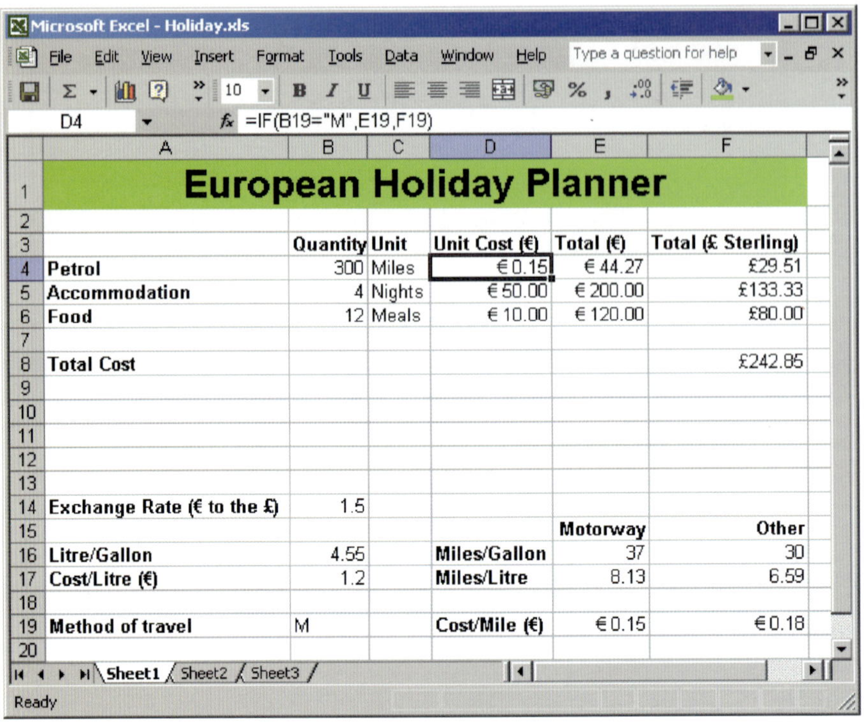

Microsoft Excel - Holiday.xls

D4 =IF(B19="M",E19,F19)

	A	B	C	D	E	F
1	European Holiday Planner					
2						
3		Quantity	Unit	Unit Cost (€)	Total (€)	Total (£ Sterling)
4	Petrol	300	Miles	€ 0.15	€ 44.27	£29.51
5	Accommodation	4	Nights	€ 50.00	€ 200.00	£133.33
6	Food	12	Meals	€ 10.00	€ 120.00	£80.00
7						
8	Total Cost					£242.85
9						
10						
11						
12						
13						
14	Exchange Rate (€ to the £)	1.5				
15					Motorway	Other
16	Litre/Gallon	4.55		Miles/Gallon	37	30
17	Cost/Litre (€)	1.2		Miles/Litre	8.13	6.59
18						
19	Method of travel	M		Cost/Mile (€)	€0.15	€0.18
20						

Figure 2.6

Type the letter O in cell B19 and press Enter. The value in cell D4, and the total cost, will change.

Remember to save your work frequently!

Setting a budget

Now you know how much it will cost, you need to compare this with how much you have to spend.

In cell A9 type Budget.

Enter a budget of £240 in cell F9.

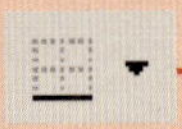

Select cells A9 to F9 and add a Bottom Border using the Borders button.

- Shade cells A10 to F10 **Light Green** using the **Fill** button.

- In cell F10 insert the formula **=F9-F8** to give you the difference between your budget and the actual cost.

Formatting negative numbers

- Click in cell F10 and select **Format**, **Cells...** from the main menu.
- Select **Currency** from the **Category** menu and choose the 2nd option from the **Negative numbers** menu. This means negative numbers will be displayed in red.

Now you can use an IF statement to display **Over Budget** in cell A10 if the number in cell F10 is negative, or **Within Budget** if the number is greater than or equal zero. Try this on your own!

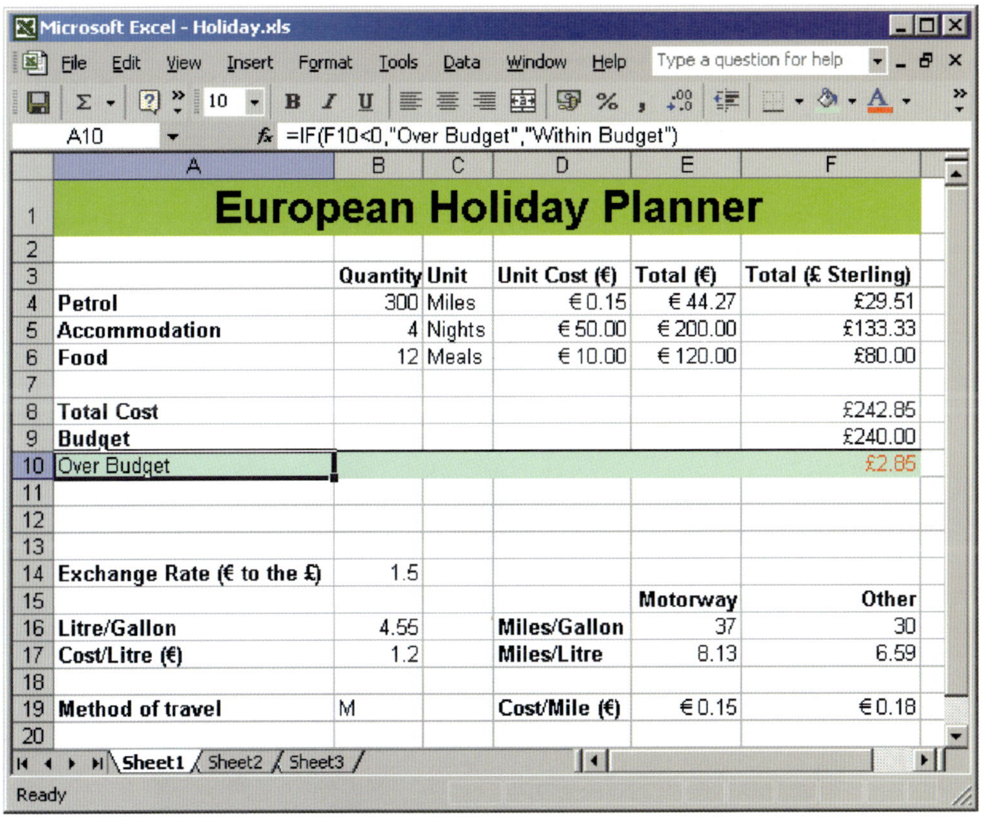

	A	B	C	D	E	F
1	European Holiday Planner					
2						
3		Quantity	Unit	Unit Cost (€)	Total (€)	Total (£ Sterling)
4	Petrol	300	Miles	€ 0.15	€ 44.27	£29.51
5	Accommodation	4	Nights	€ 50.00	€ 200.00	£133.33
6	Food	12	Meals	€ 10.00	€ 120.00	£80.00
7						
8	Total Cost					£242.85
9	Budget					£240.00
10	Over Budget					£2.85
11						
12						
13						
14	Exchange Rate (€ to the £)	1.5				
15					Motorway	Other
16	Litre/Gallon	4.55		Miles/Gallon	37	30
17	Cost/Litre (€)	1.2		Miles/Litre	8.13	6.59
18						
19	Method of travel	M		Cost/Mile (€)	€ 0.15	€ 0.18
20						

Figure 2.7

Testing your formulae

You need to test out the formulae by entering different numbers.

- Try entering £250 for the Budget figure. Which cells change?
- Now enter 0 for the method of travel. Which cells change?
- Suppose your budget is only £200. Try changing some of the expenses until your holiday comes within budget. You might have to go a bit hungry...

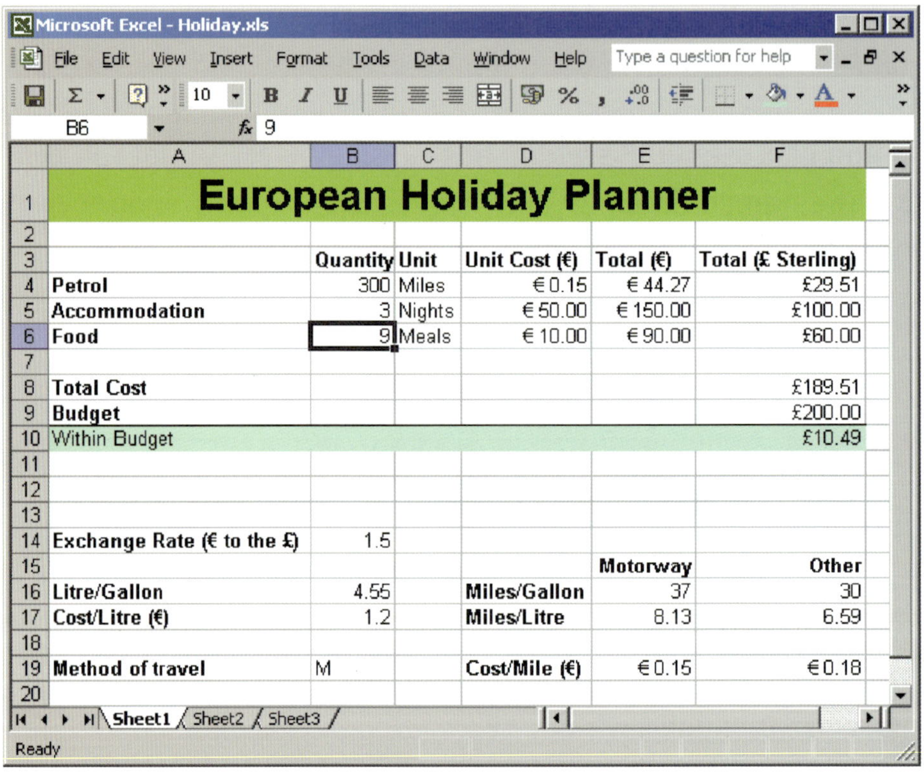

	A	B	C	D	E	F
1	European Holiday Planner					
2						
3		Quantity	Unit	Unit Cost (€)	Total (€)	Total (£ Sterling)
4	Petrol	300	Miles	€ 0.15	€ 44.27	£29.51
5	Accommodation	3	Nights	€ 50.00	€ 150.00	£100.00
6	Food	9	Meals	€ 10.00	€ 90.00	£60.00
7						
8	Total Cost					£189.51
9	Budget					£200.00
10	Within Budget					£10.49
11						
12						
13						
14	Exchange Rate (€ to the £)	1.5				
15					Motorway	Other
16	Litre/Gallon	4.55		Miles/Gallon	37	30
17	Cost/Litre (€)	1.2		Miles/Litre	8.13	6.59
18						
19	Method of travel	M		Cost/Mile (€)	€ 0.15	€ 0.18
20						

Figure 2.8: Planning to stay within a budget

- Save and close your workbook.

Documenting a Project

Chapter three 3

When you have completed a project, you will need to write it up, describing the problem and how you solved it. This chapter will give you some useful tips!

Adding a header and footer

If you are going to print your spreadsheet, you need to make sure your name is printed on it, especially if several people are going to print similar spreadsheets.

The best place to put your name is in a header or footer. You can also put the date, the name of the file and any other useful information in the header or footer.

Information in the header and footer will not show on the spreadsheet until you look at a Print Preview, or print your worksheet.

- From the main menu select **View, Header and Footer...**
- In the Page Setup window, click the **Custom Footer** button.
- Type your name in the left hand section. Click in the middle section and press the **Filename** button to insert the filename. (See figure 3.1.)
- Click in the right hand section and click the **Date** button.

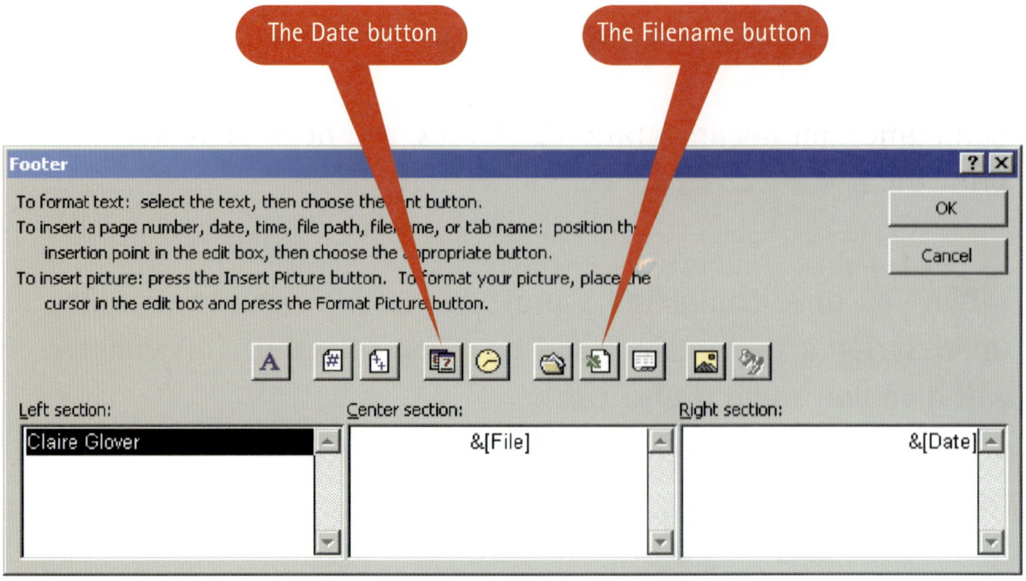

Figure 3.1: Inserting a custom footer

Click **OK**.

The Page Setup window shows you what your footer will look like.

You can experiment with some of the other options.

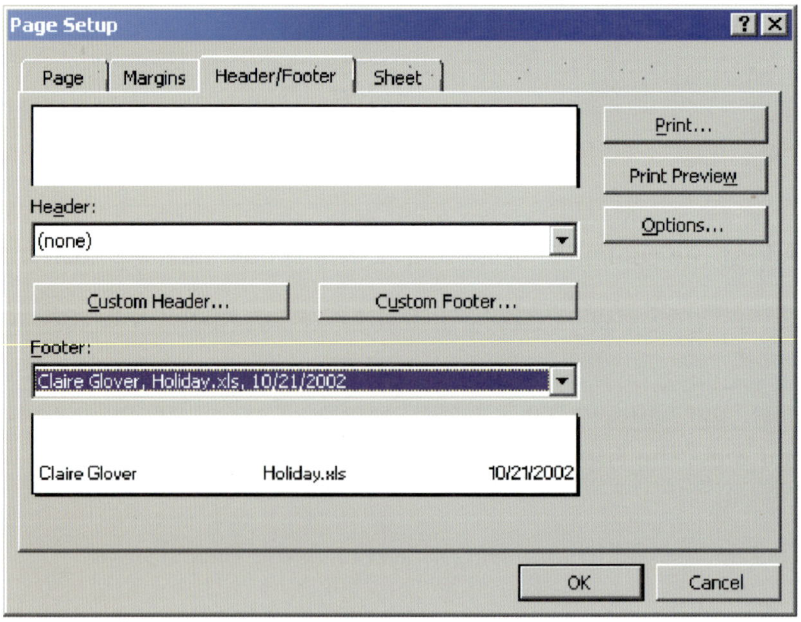

Figure 3.2: Inserting a footer

Click **OK**.

Displaying formulae

Sometimes, for documentation purposes, you need to be able to print the formulae in your worksheet.

- From the menu bar select **Tools, Options.**
- Check the **Formulas** box near the bottom of the screen.

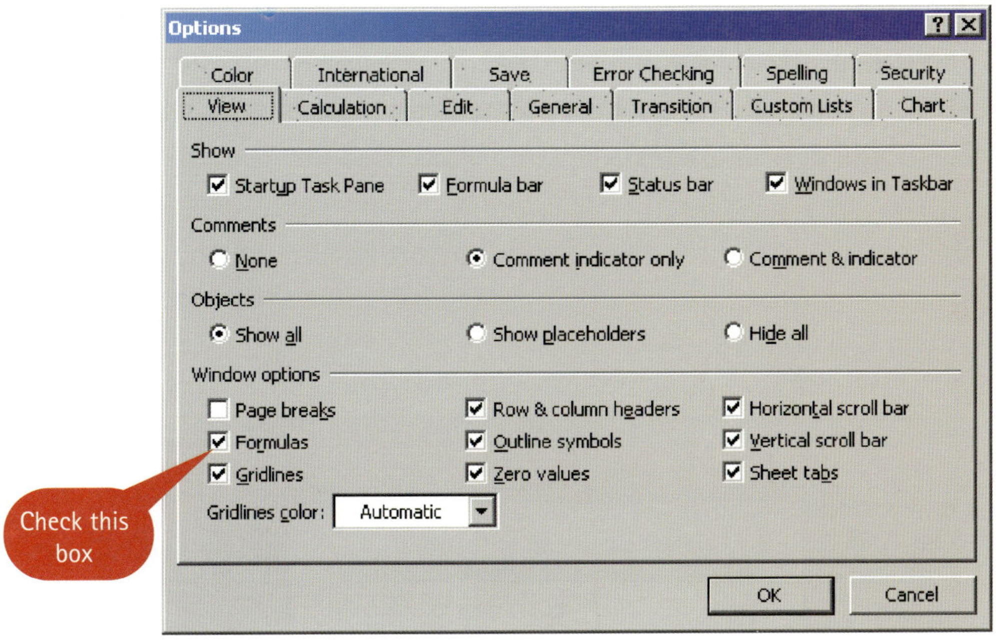

Figure 3.3

- Click **OK**.
- Adjust the column widths. Your screen should look like this:

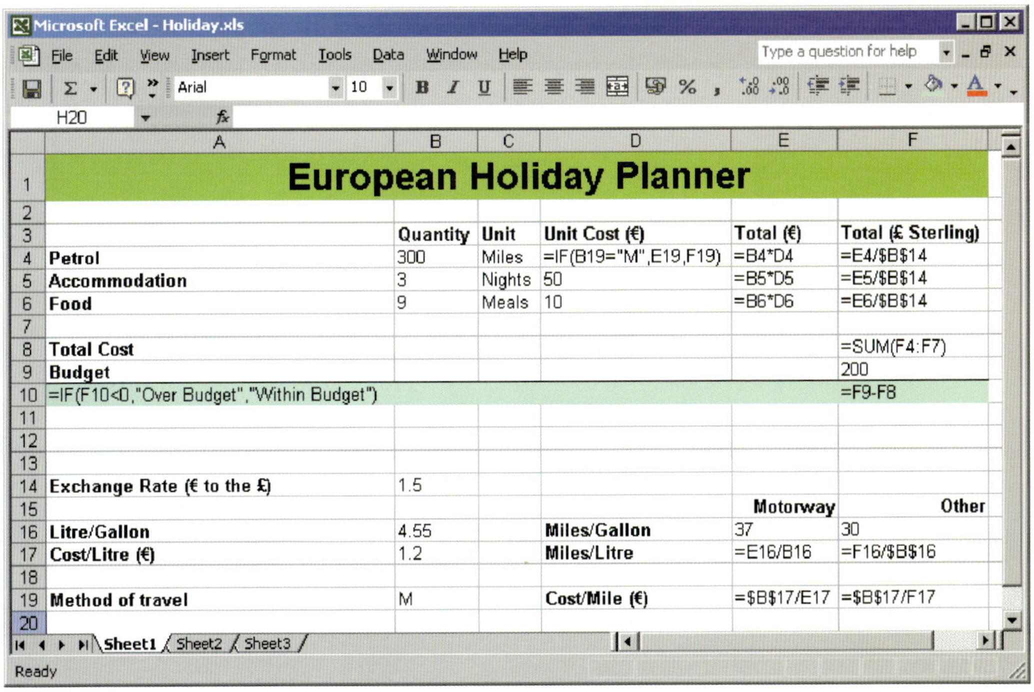

Microsoft Excel - Holiday.xls

	A	B	C	D	E	F
1	European Holiday Planner					
2						
3		Quantity	Unit	Unit Cost (€)	Total (€)	Total (£ Sterling)
4	Petrol	300	Miles	=IF(B19="M",E19,F19)	=B4*D4	=E4/$B$14
5	Accommodation	3	Nights	50	=B5*D5	=E5/$B$14
6	Food	9	Meals	10	=B6*D6	=E6/$B$14
7						
8	Total Cost					=SUM(F4:F7)
9	Budget					200
10	=IF(F10<0,"Over Budget","Within Budget")					=F9-F8
11						
12						
13						
14	Exchange Rate (€ to the £)	1.5				
15					Motorway	Other
16	Litre/Gallon	4.55		Miles/Gallon	37	30
17	Cost/Litre (€)	1.2		Miles/Litre	=E16/B16	=F16/$B$16
18						
19	Method of travel	M		Cost/Mile (€)	=$B$17/E17	=$B$17/F17
20						

Figure 3.4: Displaying formulae

Printing your formulae

- Select cells A1 to F19 by dragging across them.
- From the menu select **File**, **Print Area**, **Set Print Area**.

- Click the **Print Preview** button.

The Print Preview will show you what the spreadsheet will look like when it is printed. You will see that it will not fit on the page in Portrait layout. At the bottom of the screen Excel tells you that this is **Page 1 of 2** pages.

Note that you can press the **Zoom** button to enlarge the preview.

Can you see your footer?

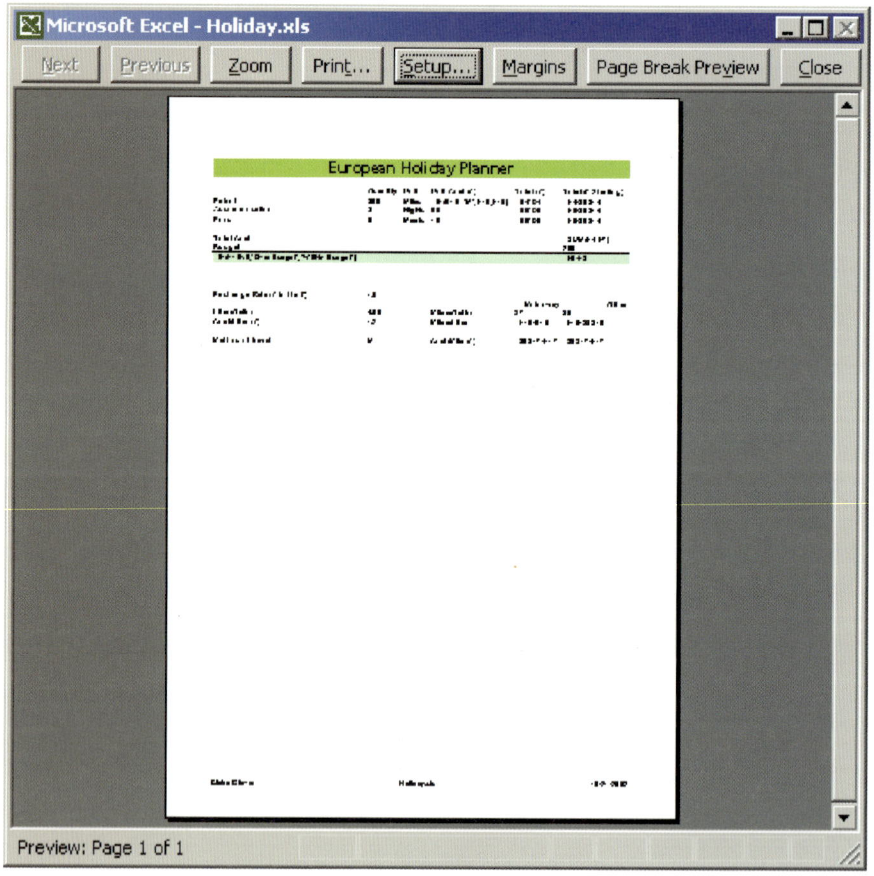

Figure 3.5

- In this window, click the **Setup** button.

You will see the Page Setup window appear.

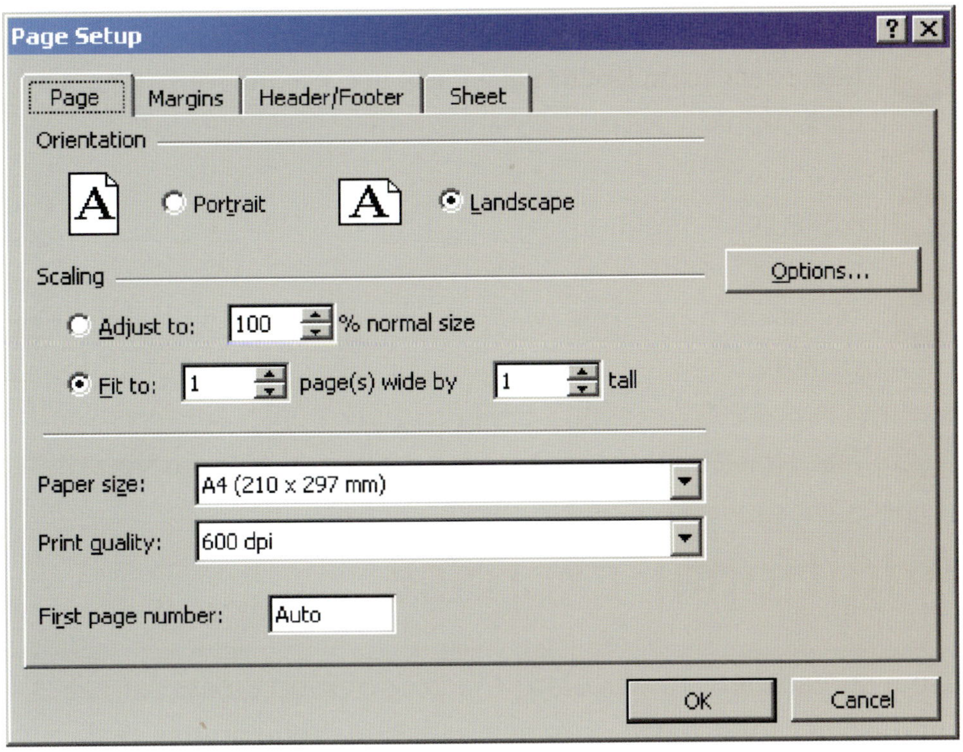

Figure 3.6: Changing the Page Setup

You have 2 options to fit the spreadsheet on to one page. You can either leave the layout as Portrait and click the **Fit to** button, to fit to 1 page wide by 1 page tall, or you can click the Landscape button.

- Experiment with each of these options.
- In the Preview window, click the **Print** button when you are ready to print, or click the **Close** button if you do not want to print yet. This will return you to the spreadsheet.

Restoring the spreadsheet

- Now select Tools, Options again and uncheck the Formulas option. Click OK.
- Adjust column widths.
- You can do a Print Preview of the spreadsheet and print it out if you want to.
- That completes this exercise, so save and close your workbook.

Additional exercise

Use a spreadsheet to calculate the cost of ingredients for cakes and biscuits for a party or to sell at a fête. You can use real recipes, putting in the amount of ingredients required, and the number of cakes or biscuits this will make. Then work out the unit cost per item. Will it be cheaper to make a large quantity? Will you have some ingredients left over?

If you are selling the cakes and biscuits, work out how much you should charge to make a reasonable profit. What if you have some left over?

Before you start work at the computer, you should use paper and pencil to plan how you are going to set out the spreadsheet. That's probably the hardest part!

Chapter 4

Modelling

In this chapter you will build a financial model for a summer ice cream sales job. The model will calculate the costs of setting up an ice cream stand and work out the profit over 2 months.

Planning the model

The first step is to decide

- what the overhead costs are. Overhead costs do not vary with sales – they include things like equipment rental.
- what you are going to sell. This could include ice cream and ice lollies, for example.

Next you need to find out how much these things will cost.

- How much is the rental of equipment for the summer (say, 60 days)? These are the fixed costs - the overheads.
- How much will you have to pay for each box of ice creams, and for each box of ice lollies? These are the variable costs, or unit costs.

Then you have to make an estimate of how many of each product you think you might sell. This will probably vary according to the weather, so your model can take this into account.

You will be able to use your model to see how much profit you will make over a good summer or a bad summer.
You can see how the profit is affected by changing the price of ice cream, or by choosing a better pitch and selling more.

Building the Model

- Open **Microsoft Excel**.
- In a new worksheet, enter the text shown in Figure 4.1.
- Highlight all the text and make it **Bold**. Colour the text in the selected areas blue.
- The headings in rows 9 and 14 need to be right-justified.
- You will need to alter column widths to make your spreadsheet look like the one in the figure.

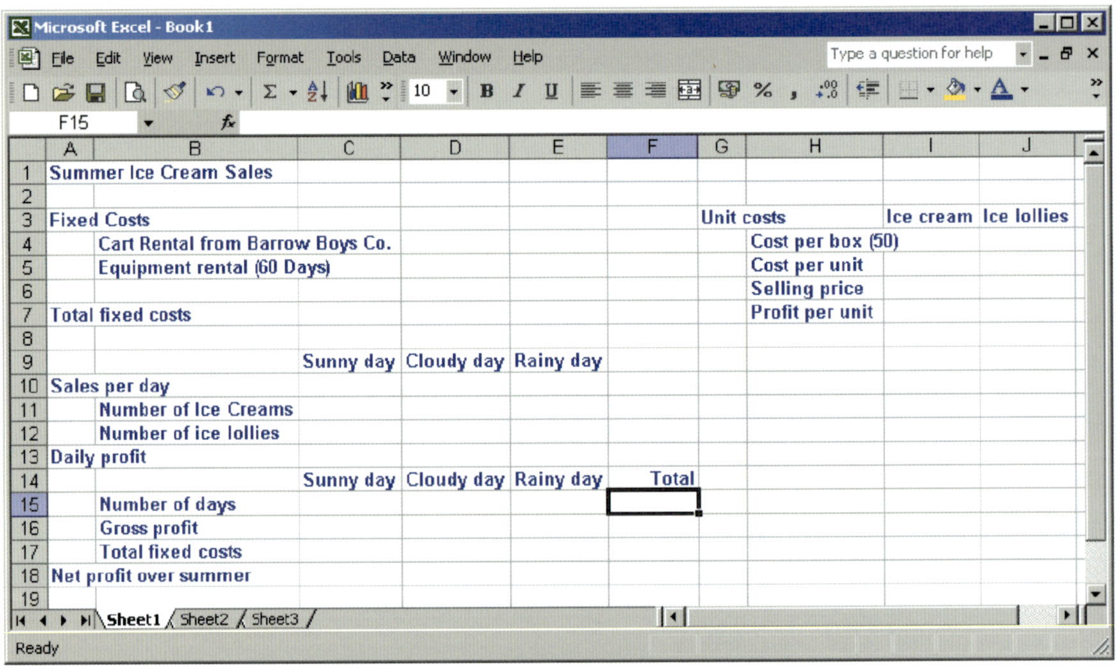

Figure 4.1

> **Tip:**
> To select all the headings, hold down Ctrl while you select different blocks of cells.

- Merge and centre the title 'Summer Ice Cream Sales' over cells A1 to J1 and increase the **Font Size** to **20**.
- Save your workbook as **Ice Cream Sales.xls**.

Entering estimated figures

The next step in building the model is to enter the fixed costs and unit costs. Then enter some estimates for how many sunny days, cloudy days and rainy days you think might occur, and the number of ice creams and lollies you might sell in a day. Decide how much you will charge for ice creams and lollies.

- Enter figures as shown in Figure 4.2. Select all the areas shown, which will contain amounts of money, and press the Currency button to format them all as Currency.

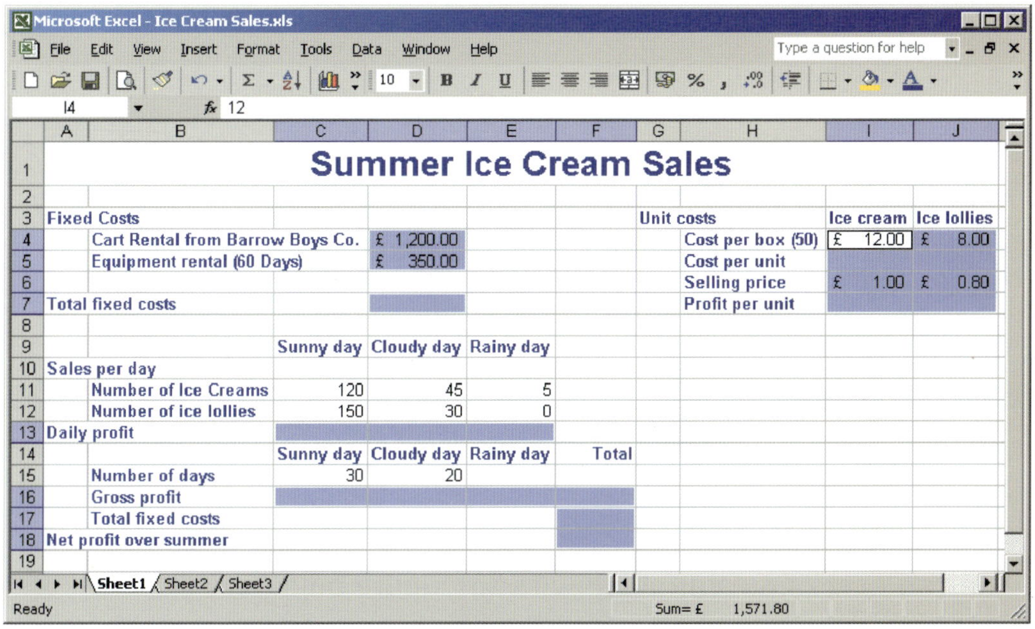

	A	B	C	D	E	F	G	H	I	J
1			Summer Ice Cream Sales							
2										
3	Fixed Costs						Unit costs		Ice cream	Ice lollies
4		Cart Rental from Barrow Boys Co.		£ 1,200.00				Cost per box (50)	£ 12.00	£ 8.00
5		Equipment rental (60 Days)		£ 350.00				Cost per unit		
6								Selling price	£ 1.00	£ 0.80
7	Total fixed costs							Profit per unit		
8										
9			Sunny day	Cloudy day	Rainy day					
10	Sales per day									
11		Number of Ice Creams	120	45	5					
12		Number of ice lollies	150	30	0					
13	Daily profit									
14			Sunny day	Cloudy day	Rainy day	Total				
15		Number of days	30	20						
16		Gross profit								
17		Total fixed costs								
18	Net profit over summer									
19										

Figure 4.2

Entering the formulae

Now you need to work out all the formulae to put in the model.

- In cell D7, enter the formula for Total fixed costs.
- In cell I5, enter a formula for the cost per ice cream, assuming there are 50 ice creams in a box.
- Copy this formula to cell J5.

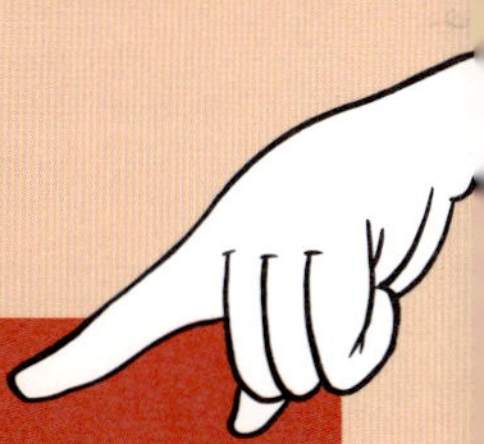

Tip:
Start all formulae with an = sign. You can 'point' at a cell instead of typing it in a formula.

Enter formulae for the profit on each ice cream and ice lolly.

In cell C13, you need to enter a formula for the daily profit, and then copy this formula to cells D13 and E13. Be careful – the profit per unit needs to be entered as an **absolute** reference, not a **relative** reference!

When you have entered all the formulae, you should get figures as shown in Figure 4.3.

Ice Cream Sales.xls

	A	B	C	D	E	F	G	H	I	J
1				Summer Ice Cream Sales						
2										
3	Fixed Costs						Unit costs		Ice cream	Ice lollies
4		Cart Rental from Barrow Boys Co.		£ 1,200.00				Cost per box (50)	£ 12.00	£ 8.00
5		Equipment rental (60 Days)		£ 350.00				Cost per unit	£ 0.24	£ 0.16
6								Selling price	£ 1.00	£ 0.80
7	Total fixed costs			£ 1,550.00				Profit per unit	£ 0.76	£ 0.64
8										
9			Sunny day	Cloudy day	Rainy day					
10	Sales per day									
11		Number of Ice Creams	120	45	5					
12		Number of ice lollies	150	30	0					
13	Daily profit		£ 187.20	£ 53.40	£ 3.80					
14			Sunny day	Cloudy day	Rainy day	Total				
15		Number of days	30	20	10					
16		Gross profit	£5,616.00	£ 1,068.00	£ 38.00	£6,722.00				
17		Total fixed costs				£1,550.00				
18	Net profit over summer					£5,172.00				

Sheet1 / Sheet2 / Sheet3

Figure 4.3: The completed model

You can check your formulae with the figure below.

Ice Cream Sales.xls

	A	B	C	D	E	F	G	H	I	J
1				Summer Ice Cream Sales						
2										
3	Fixed (						Unit cc		Ice cream	Ice lollies
4		Cart Re		1200				Cost pe	12	8
5		Equipm		350				Cost pe	=I4/50	=J4/50
6								Selling	1	0.8
7	Total fi			=SUM(D4:D5)				Profit p	=I6-I5	=J6-J5
8										
9			Sunny day	Cloudy day	Rainy day					
10	Sales p									
11		Numbe	120	45	5					
12		Numbe	150	30	0					
13	Daily p		=C11*$I$7+C12*$J$7	=D11*$I$7+D12*$J$7	=E11*$I$7+E12*$J$7					
14			Sunny day	Cloudy day	Rainy day	Total				
15		Numbe	30	20	=60-C15-D15					
16		Gross p	=C15*C13	=D15*D13	=E15*E13	=SUM(C16:E16)				
17		Total fi				=D7				
18	Net pro					=F16-F17				

Sheet1 / Sheet2 / Sheet3

Figure 4.4: The formulae

Tip:
To make I7 an absolute reference, type $I$7 in the formula. Or, enter the reference in the formula by pointing to I7, then pressing the function key F4.

Tip:
Enter a formula, not a value, in cell E15. The summer job is for 60 days, so enter **=60-C15-D15**.

Naming Cells

To make it easier for you to read the formulae in your spreadsheet, it is often a good idea to give the cells meaningful names rather than using the cell reference.

- Click on cell F18.

The name **'F18'** will appear the Name Box in the top-left hand corner of the screen. (Just above column A.)

- Select Insert, Name, Define... from the main menu.
- Type NetProfit and click OK.

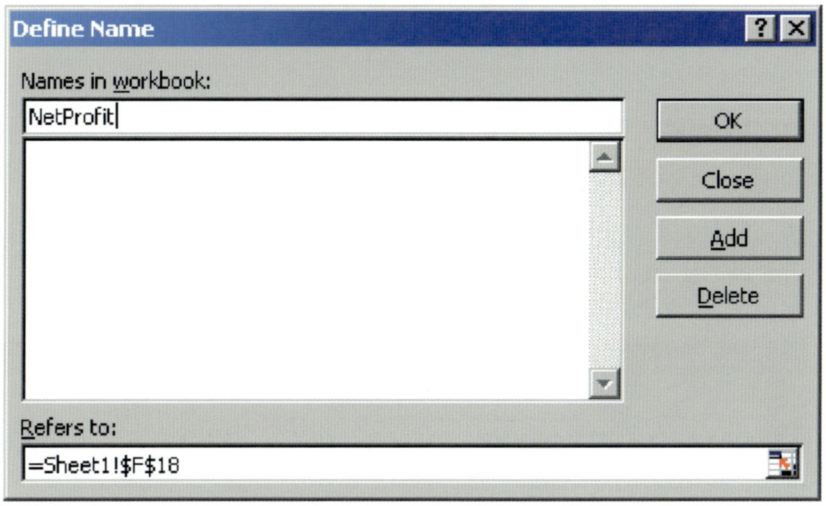

Figure 4.5: Naming a cell

The name in the Name Box should change to say NetProfit.

- Name cell D7 TotalFixedCosts.
- Delete the contents of cell F17 and type =TotalFixedCosts.

You should see the same result as before but the formula is now easier to understand.

- Name cells C15, D15 and E15, SunnyDays, CloudyDays and RainyDays.

Tip:
There is an even easier way to name a selected cell. Just click in the **Name** box (see Figure 1.1) and type the name. Then press **Enter**. Spaces are not allowed in a cell name.

If...then...else

You have already used an 'If' function in Chapter 2. It allows you to show different values in one cell depending on a value in another.

Suppose that you have decided that if you cannot make at least £1500 net profit, it is not worth the risk.

This logic works like this: If I make enough money then I have a job, else I find something new. You can apply this to your worksheet.

- Click the mouse in cell B20 and type Project Outcome.

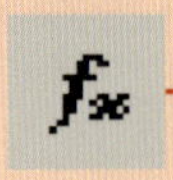

- Click in cell C20 and select More Functions from the drop-down list on the AutoSum button.
- Select Logical from the Function category and IF as the Function name. Click OK.
- Type in the instructions in the window below:

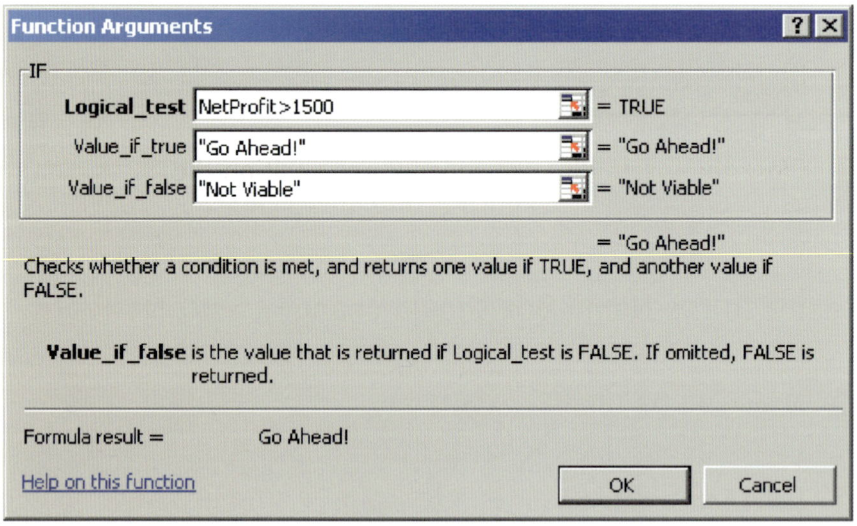

Figure 4.6

- Click OK.
- Save the worksheet.

Adding Clip Art

You can make your spreadsheet look quite cheery by adding clip art, using coloured text and shading, and removing gridlines.

- Select a blank cell.
- Click on **Insert**, **Picture**, **Clip Art...**
- In the **Search** box type **ice cream**. Press **Enter**.

Figure 4.7: Searching for Clip Art

- Double-click the ice-cream picture.
- Close the **Insert Clip Art** window and position the graphic on your worksheet.

Note:

You may need to have the MS Office XP CD in the drive.

Removing gridlines

Removing the gridlines can sometimes improve the appearance of your spreadsheet.

From the menu select Tools, Options. Click the View tab. Uncheck Gridlines and click OK.

Using colour

Tip:
Shade in turquoise the cells containing numbers but none of the cells containing formulae.

Next, you might like to use shading and text colour to brighten up the spreadsheet. In the figure below, all the cells where you can change figures without altering the basic model have been shaded turquoise.

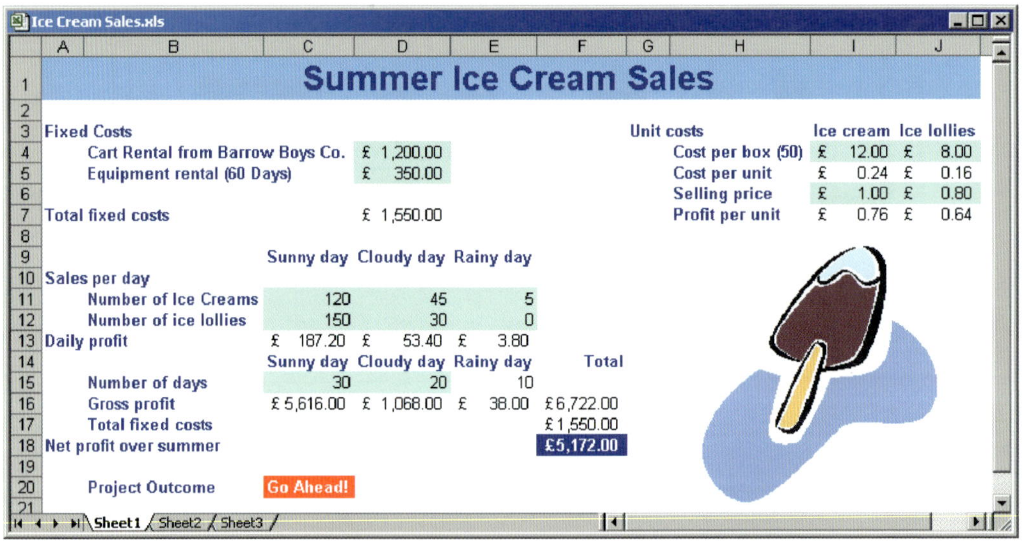

Figure 4.8: Adding some colour

Save your spreadsheet again.

What if...?

What ifs? enable you to enter different values for costs and revenues to see their effects on the rest of the spreadsheet and, of course, the net profit.

For example you should now see that in cell C20 there is the text "Go Ahead!". But what if it is a bad summer with few sunny days? What if the cost of a box of ice creams increased to £15?

- Reduce the number of sunny days to 10. What happens?
- What if your equipment hire increased to £600 but you decided that you could get away with charging an extra 10p per ice cream and ice lolly?

With your spreadsheet looking like the screenshot below, try out some figures to see how much you could reduce the price of ice lollies for the project to remain viable. Restore the price to 90p afterwards.

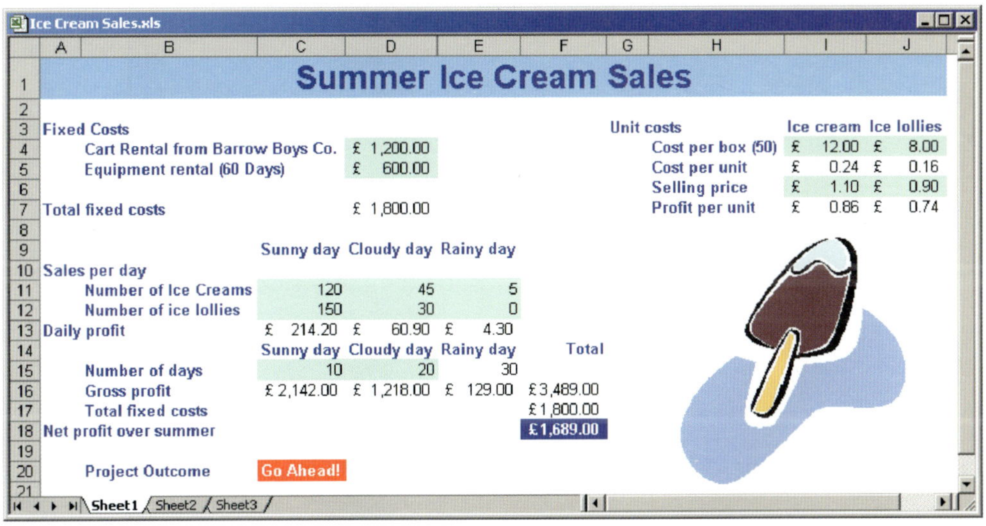
Ice Cream Sales.xls

	A/B	C	D	E	F	H	I	J
1	Summer Ice Cream Sales							
2								
3	Fixed Costs					Unit costs	Ice cream	Ice lollies
4	Cart Rental from Barrow Boys Co.		£ 1,200.00			Cost per box (50)	£ 12.00	£ 8.00
5	Equipment rental (60 Days)		£ 600.00			Cost per unit	£ 0.24	£ 0.16
6						Selling price	£ 1.10	£ 0.90
7	Total fixed costs		£ 1,800.00			Profit per unit	£ 0.86	£ 0.74
8								
9		Sunny day	Cloudy day	Rainy day				
10	Sales per day							
11	Number of Ice Creams	120	45	5				
12	Number of ice lollies	150	30	0				
13	Daily profit	£ 214.20	£ 60.90	£ 4.30				
14		Sunny day	Cloudy day	Rainy day	Total			
15	Number of days	10	20	30				
16	Gross profit	£ 2,142.00	£ 1,218.00	£ 129.00	£3,489.00			
17	Total fixed costs				£1,800.00			
18	Net profit over summer				£1,689.00			
19								
20	Project Outcome	Go Ahead!						

Sheet1 / Sheet2 / Sheet3

Figure 4.9: Is the project viable?

Protecting your worksheet

To help prevent you from accidentally changing any of the formulae, you can lock all the cells that you don't need to change. This is sometimes particularly helpful when you are creating a spreadsheet that someone else is likely to use.

To do this, you first have to unlock all the cells that can be changed. This is all the cells shaded in turquoise.

- Hold down the Control key (Ctrl on your keyboard) and select the cells highlighted in figure 4.8. This will make a multiple selection.
- Select Format, Cells... from the main menu.
- Click the Protection tab and uncheck the Locked option.
- Click OK.

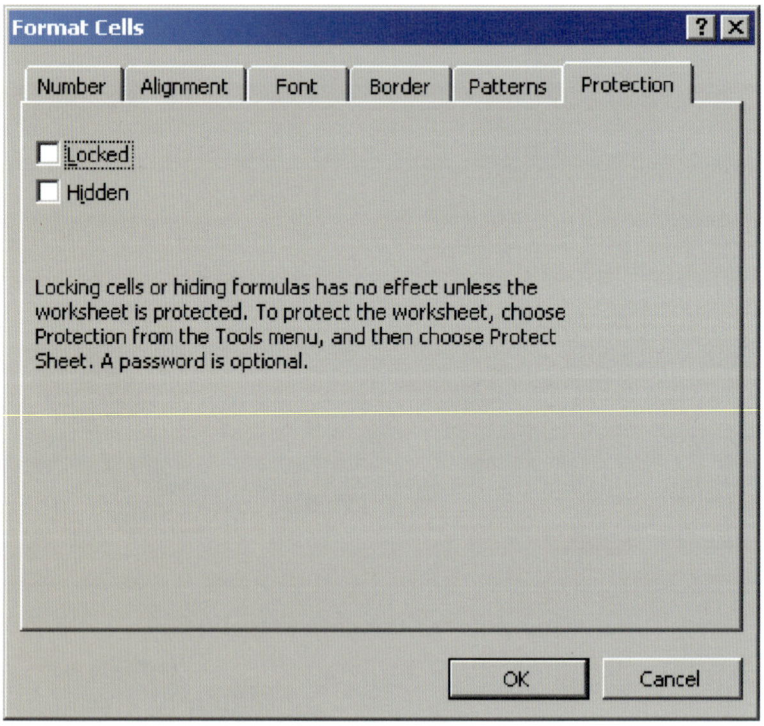

Figure 4.10: Unlocking cells

Now you can protect the entire worksheet, leaving only the unlocked cells available for editing.

- Click anywhere on the worksheet to deselect the highlighted cells.

Select **Tools**, **Protection**, **Protect Sheet...** from the main menu.

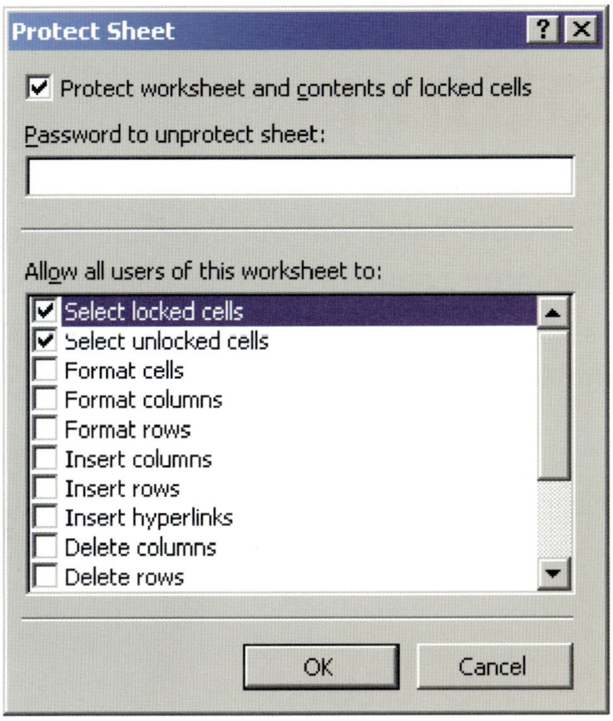

Figure 4.11: Protecting a worksheet

Click **OK**.

Try making a change in any cell not shaded turquoise. You will find you can't!

If you need to change a formula in your worksheet, you can do so by first selecting **Tools**, **Protection** from the menu and then clicking **Unprotect Sheet**.

Save your workbook, close it and take a break!

Tip:

It is a good idea not to enter a password because you will probably not be able to remember it next week!

Chapter 5

Formatting

In the next two chapters you will build a table to hold the results of a Badminton competition. Five teams are entering, and each team plays all the other teams once. A team scores 1 for a Win and 0 for a Loss.

You can look a few pages ahead to Figure 5.8 to see what the final table will look like. You'll be learning a few formatting tricks along the way!

Starting the table

- Start Excel and a new blank worksheet will appear on your screen.
- Enter the following headings, without altering any column widths:

	A	B	C
1	Badminton Tournament		
2			
3	Team	Angels	
4		Buffalos	
5		Crimsons	
6		Dreadnoughts	
7		Eagles	
8		Fliers	
9			

Figure 5.1: The teams in the tournament

Copy and Paste Special

The team names need to be copied to row 2. You can copy them as follows:

- Select cells B3 to B8, right-click and select **Copy**.
- Right-click in cell C2 and select **Paste Special**.
- Click **Transpose** in the **Paste Special** window.

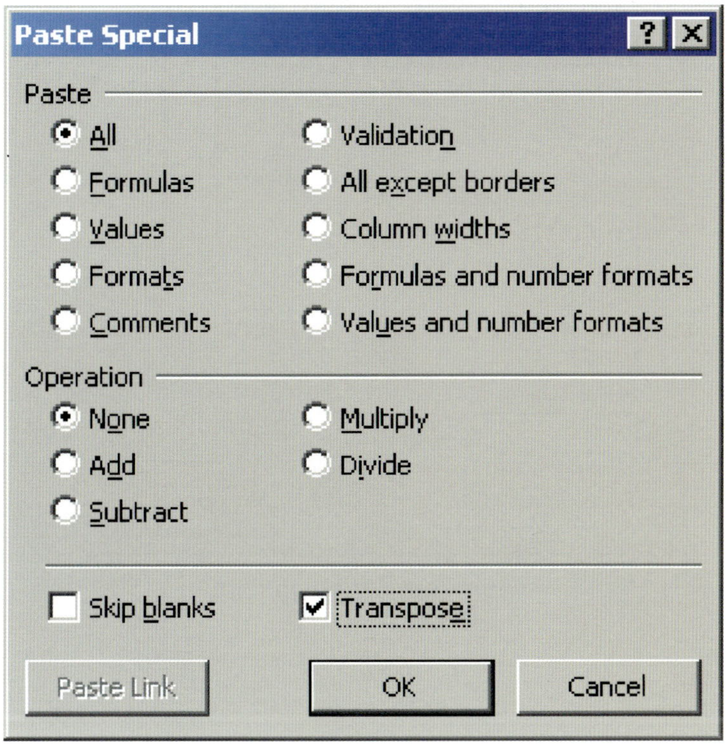

Figure 5.2: The Paste Special window

- Click **OK**.
- Press **Esc** to get rid of the dotted line around the cells you selected and end the operation.
- Select all the headings (hold down **Ctrl** while you select different areas) and make them all bold.

Tip:
Paste Special is a very useful option. Take a look at all the other things you can do. Some of them will come in useful!

Wrapping text

- Select cells A1 to B2. Change the font size to 16.
- From the menu select Format, Cells...
- Click the Alignment tab. As in the screenshot below, set Horizontal and Vertical to Center, and check Wrap Text and Merge cells.

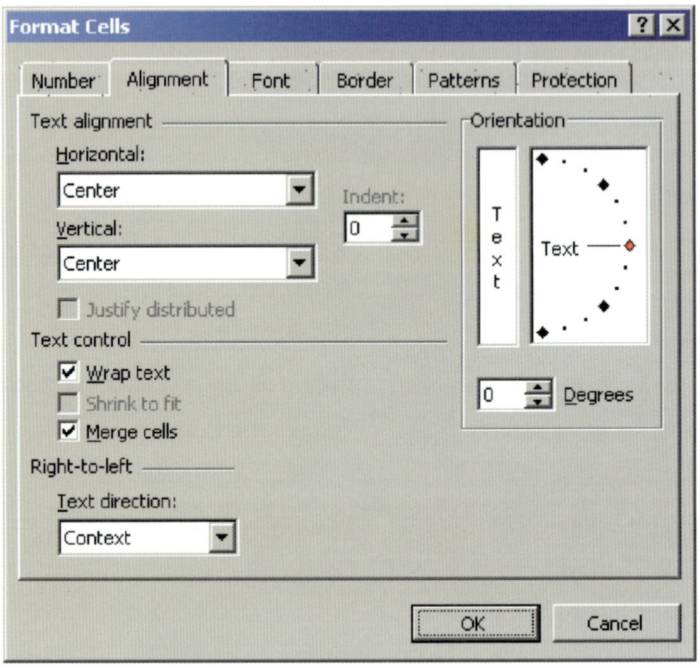

Figure 5.3: Wrapping text

- Click OK.
- The text will overflow the cells. Drag the border between row headers 2 and 3 to make the row deep enough.

Figure 5.4

- Widen column B just enough to fit Tournament and Dreadnoughts without overflowing.

Changing text orientation

The team names don't fit neatly in the cells in row 2. Of course, you could widen the columns but you can practise another neat trick.

- Select cells C2 to H2. Select **Format**, **Cells...** from the menu.
- The **Alignment** tab should already be selected. In the **Orientation** box, drag the red dot anti-clockwise until the box below shows **60 degrees**.
- Click **OK**. Deepen Row 2 and if necessary widen columns to fit each label.

Now your headings should look like this:

	A	B	C	D	E	F	G	H
1								
2	Badminton Tournament		Angels	Buffalos	Crimsons	Dreadnoughts	Eagles	Fliers
3	Team	Angels						
4		Buffalos						
5		Crimsons						
6		Dreadnoughts						
7		Eagles						
8		Fliers						
9								

Figure 5.5

- Next, merge and centre cells A3 to A8 and change the orientation of **Team** in cell A3. Make the text size **16**.
- Add some colour – select cells A1, C3, D4 etc. down to H8 and shade them **Pale Blue**. Shade the team names and make them **Gold**.

Make the rows in the table a bit deeper.

- Drag across row headers 3 to 8.
- Drag the border between any two row headers.

Adding borders

The table needs borders to make it easy to read when it is printed out.

- Select cells B3 to H8.
- Click the Borders button on the toolbar and select All Borders.

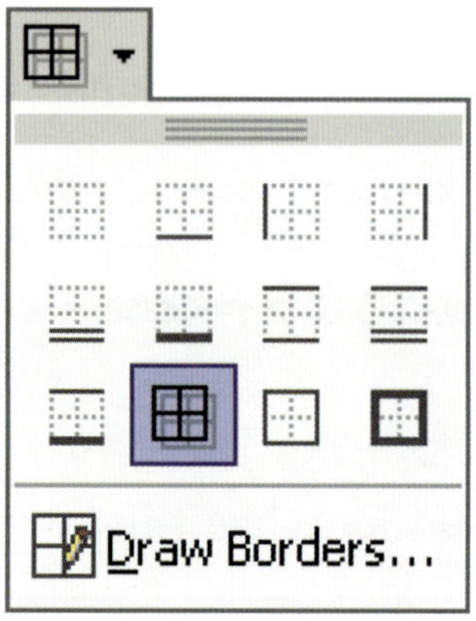

Figure 5.6: Adding borders

- Save your worksheet as Badminton.xls.

Now your worksheet should look like this:

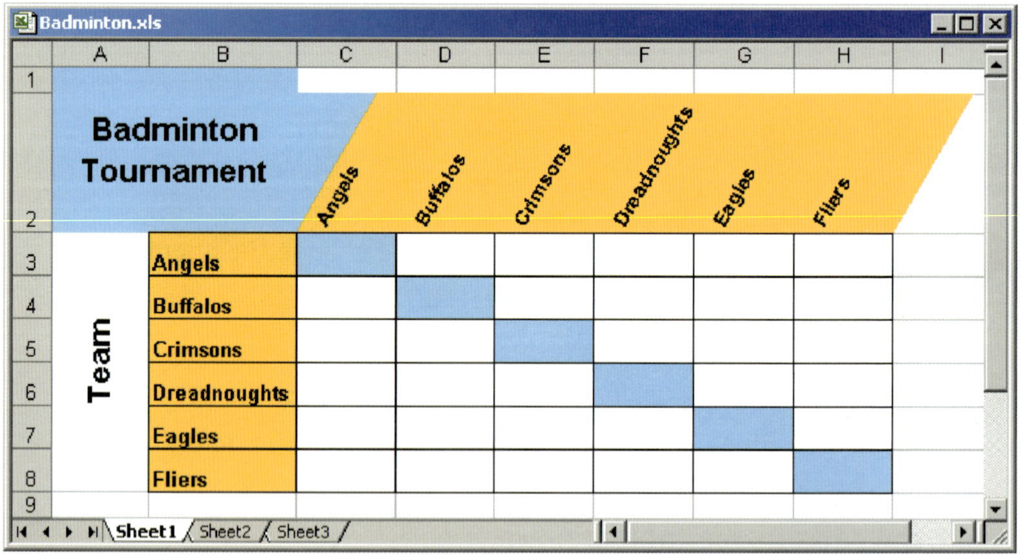

Figure 5.7: The table so far

Maybe you would like the team names centred vertically in the cells. Try selecting cells B3 to B8, right-clicking and choosing Format cells... You will recognise this window!

Test data

The next step is to enter some scores into the table. Suppose that as the tournament day progresses, the following results come in:

Angels won against Crimsons

Buffalos lost against Eagles

Crimsons won against Fliers

Angels lost against Eagles

Buffalos lost against Dreadnoughts

Fliers lost against Dreadnoughts

Each result is entered into the table twice.

- Reading across the row for Angels, enter 1 in the column for Crimsons. Then in the row for Crimsons, enter a 0 in the column for Angels.

- Enter the rest of the test data.

- Centre the results in the table both horizontally and vertically. Make the text size 16.

When you have entered all the test data, your table should look like this:

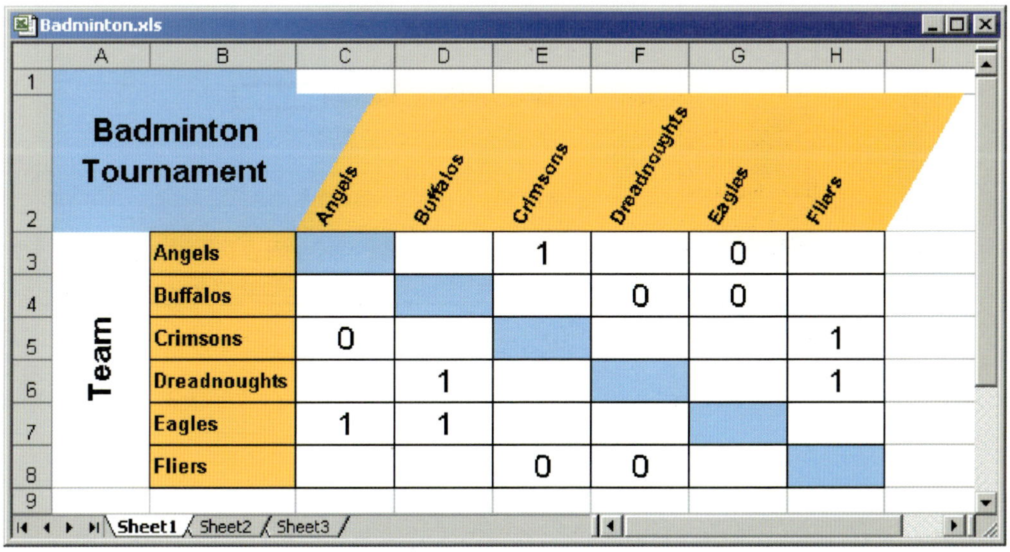

	Angels	Buffalos	Crimsons	Dreadnoughts	Eagles	Fliers
Angels			1		0	
Buffalos				0	0	
Crimsons	0					1
Dreadnoughts		1				1
Eagles	1	1				
Fliers			0	0		

Figure 5.8: Entering scores

- Save and close your table – you'll be working on it some more in the next chapter.

Chapter 6

Naming and Sorting Ranges

In this chapter you'll transfer the figures from the Badminton Tournament results table created in Chapter 5 to a new table which will show who is in the lead.

- Start Excel and open the worksheet Badminton.xls.
- Copy the team names from cells B3 to B8 to cells starting in B12.
- In cells C11 to F11 type headings Won, Lost, Played, Points.
- Shade the cells Gold and make the text bold.

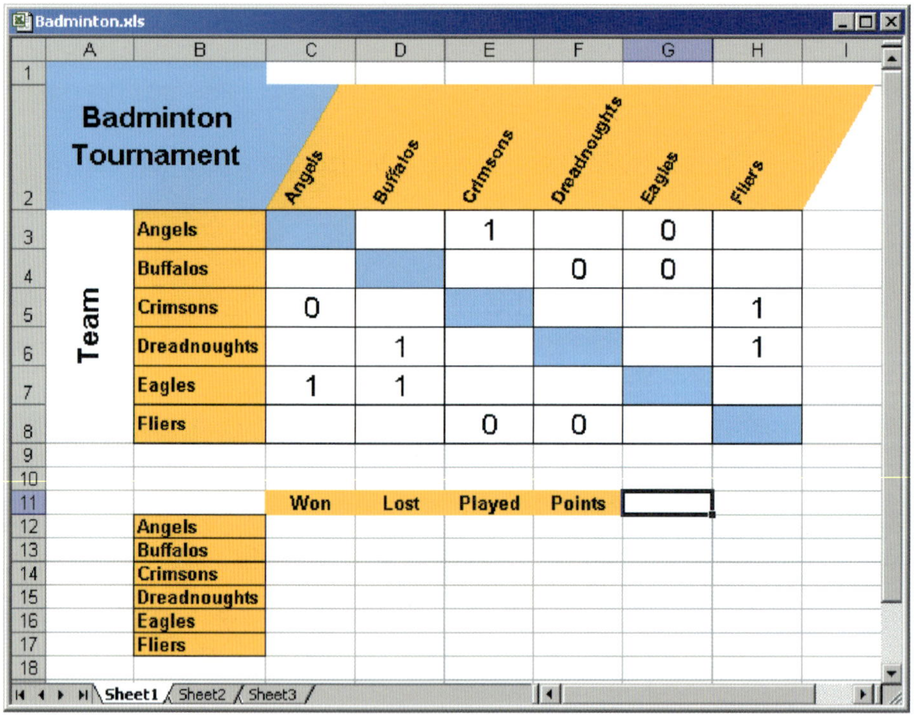

Figure 6.1

Naming cell ranges

You have already seen how to name individual cells. Now you will name a range of cells. Doing this has two advantages:

- it makes formulae referring to the ranges easier to understand.
- it means that the cells referenced are absolute references. This is important in this particular exercise because we are going to sort the Results table, and unless all the formulae in this table use absolute references, they will get muddled up when they are sorted into different positions in the table. Try it sometime!

> **Tip:** When you copy or move a formula containing an **absolute** cell reference the cell reference does not change - see Chapter 2.

- Select cells B3 to H8.
- From the menu select Insert, Name, Create.

A Create Names dialogue box will appear. Leave Left Column ticked. This will give each row in the table the name in the left column, i.e. the team name.

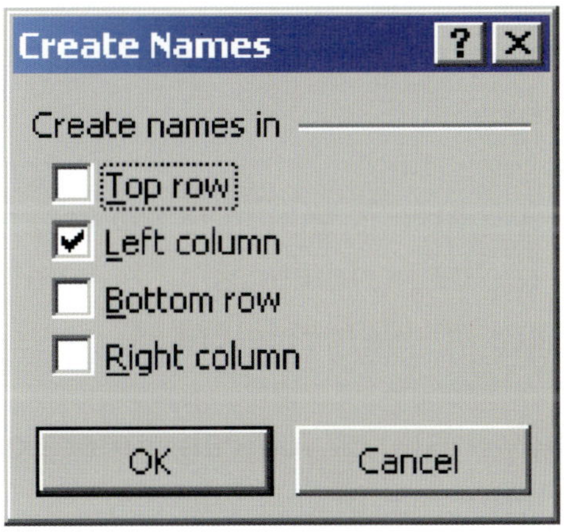

Figure 6.2

- Click OK.

Now we are going to name the columns in the second table.

- Select cells C11 to F17.
- From the menu select Insert, Name, Create.
- This time, leave Top Row selected and click OK.

Viewing and deleting cell names

You can look at all the names you have given to various cells.

If you make a mistake when naming a cell or a range of cells, you may want to delete the name.

From the menu select **Insert**, **Name**, **Define**.

The **Define Name** window appears.

Figure 6.3: Viewing cell names

Highlight any name and the range it represents appears in the **Refers to** list box.

Notice that the sheet name is shown in quotes, followed by an exclamation mark. The cell references all have dollar signs, showing that they are *absolute* references.

If you have made any mistakes you can either delete the cell names, or edit the reference in this window.

When you have finished looking at the cell names, click **Close**, or **OK** if you have made any changes.

Using range names in formulae

- In cell C12, click the Sum button and select cells C3 to H3. The formula in the Formula bar should say =Sum(Angels). Press Enter.

- Enter the correct formula e.g. =Sum(Buffalos), etc. in each of the cells C13 to C17.

Since each win is worth one point, the number of points will be the same as the number of wins.

- In cell F12, enter the formula =Won.
- Copy this formula down the column.

The Countif function

To figure out the number of games lost, you need a Countif function. This counts the number of cells containing a specified value.

- In cell D12, press the down arrow next to the AutoSum button, and click More Functions. Select Statistical in the Category list and scroll down to select Countif in the Functions list. Press OK.

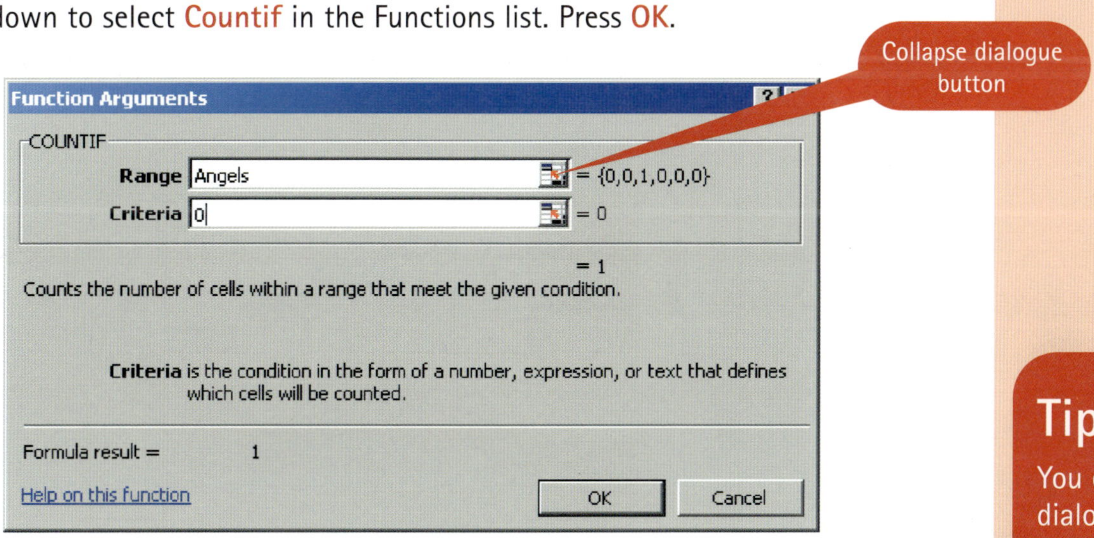

Figure 6.4: The Countif function

- Point to the Angels range or type Angels in the Range box.
- Type 0 in the Criteria box and press OK.

Tip:
Try copying this formula down the column. You will find each cell contains =Sum(Angels), which is not what you want, so **Undo** the last action.

Tip:
You can drag the dialogue box out of the way, or use the Collapse dialogue button if you can't see the Angels range to point at. Press it again to restore the window.

Editing formulae in the Formula Bar

- Copy the formula down the column by dragging the Fill handle.
- Click in cell D13.
- Double-click the word Angels in the Formula Bar and type Buffalos. Press Enter. Ignore the Inconsistent formula warning.

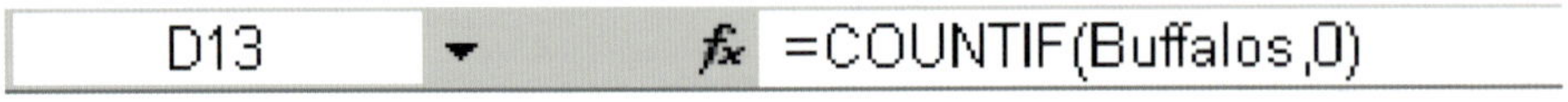

Figure 6.5: Editing an entry in the Formula Bar

- In a similar way, edit the entries in D14 to D17.

Now you can enter the formula for the number of games played. It will equal the number of games won plus the number of games lost.

- In cell E12, type =Won+lost and press Enter.
- Copy the formula down the column.
- Check your results.

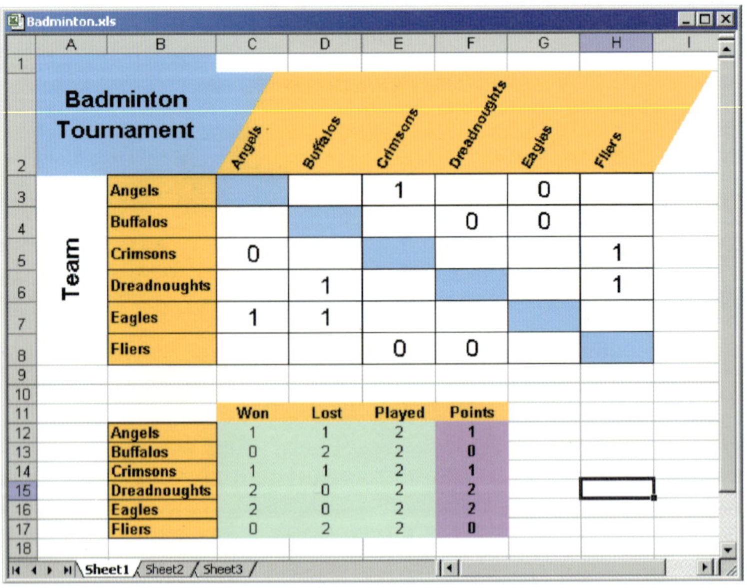

Figure 6.6

- Save your worksheet.

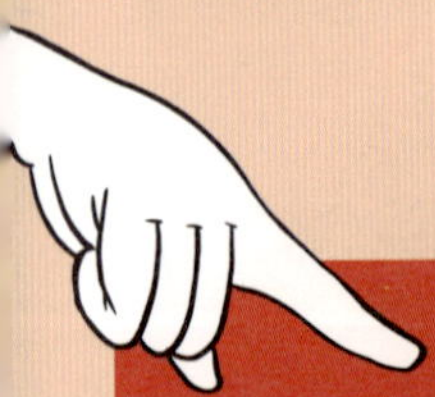

Tip:
Copying gives the wrong formula, because **Angels** is an absolute reference, but you can easily edit each formula in the Formula Bar.

Tip:
You can go a little mad with colour if you like!

Sorting

Naturally, you want the results table sorted with the current winning team at the top. We will sort in descending order of points. When two teams have the same number of points, the team who has played fewer games will come first in the table. If all else is equal, teams will be sorted in alphabetical order.

- Select cells B12 to F17.
- Select **Data**, **Sort** from the menu.
- Fill in the boxes as shown below.

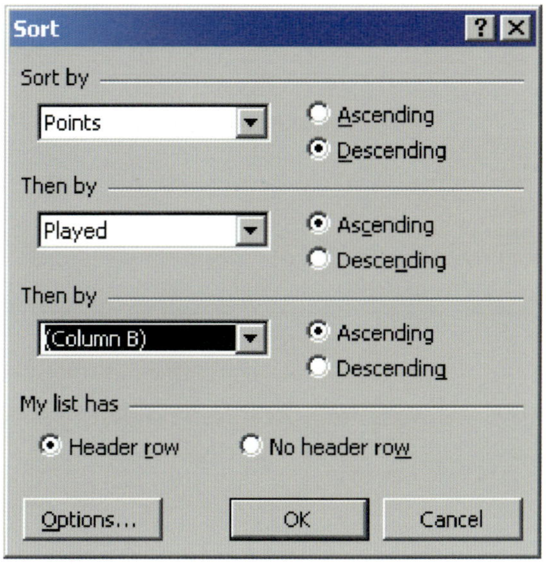

Figure 6.7

- Click **OK**. The teams should be sorted correctly.

	Won	Lost	Played	Points
Dreadnoughts	2	0	2	2
Eagles	2	0	2	2
Angels	1	1	2	1
Crimsons	1	1	2	1
Buffalos	0	2	2	0
Fliers	0	2	2	0

Figure 6.8: The sorted results table

Some more results come in... the Eagles have beaten the Crimsons, the Buffalos have beaten the Fliers and the Angels have beaten the Dreadnoughts.

Enter these results and make sure your results table is correctly updated.

Sort the table again. The Eagles are winning, the Fliers are trailing...

You can move cells around, add a heading, borders, colour, and so on. You'll end up with something like the screenshot below.

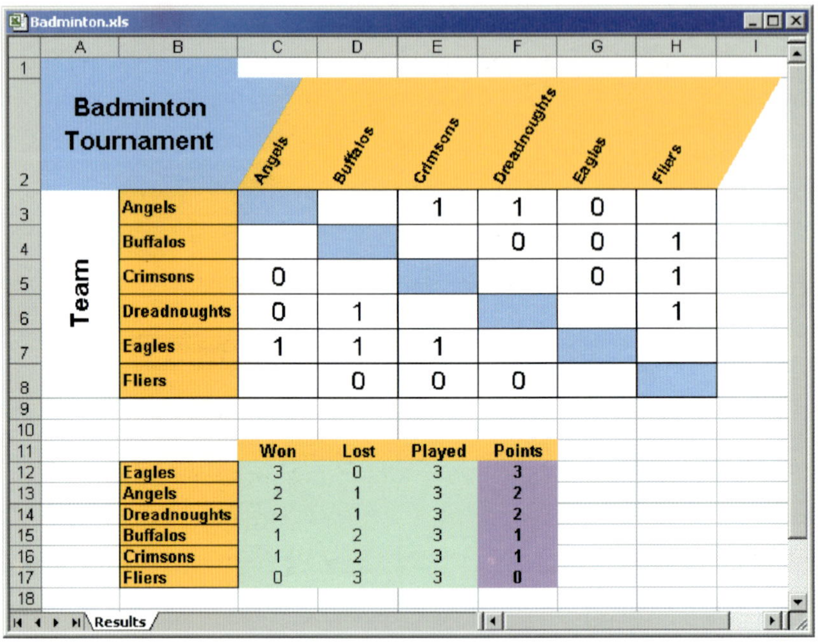

	Angels	Buffalos	Crimsons	Dreadnoughts	Eagles	Fliers
Angels			1	1	0	
Buffalos				0	0	1
Crimsons	0				0	1
Dreadnoughts	0	1				1
Eagles	1	1	1			
Fliers		0	0	0		

	Won	Lost	Played	Points
Eagles	3	0	3	3
Angels	2	1	3	2
Dreadnoughts	2	1	3	2
Buffalos	1	2	3	1
Crimsons	1	2	3	1
Fliers	0	3	3	0

Figure 6.9

You can name the worksheet **Results** and delete sheets that you have not used.

Don't forget to add your name (in a footer) and save your work before you look at it in Print Preview to make sure it fits neatly on the page.

That's it for this exercise!

Additional exercise

If you want a real challenge, try creating a table for a football or hockey league where each team plays the others twice. Home scores are recorded in the top part of the table, and Away scores in the bottom part. Draws are possible.

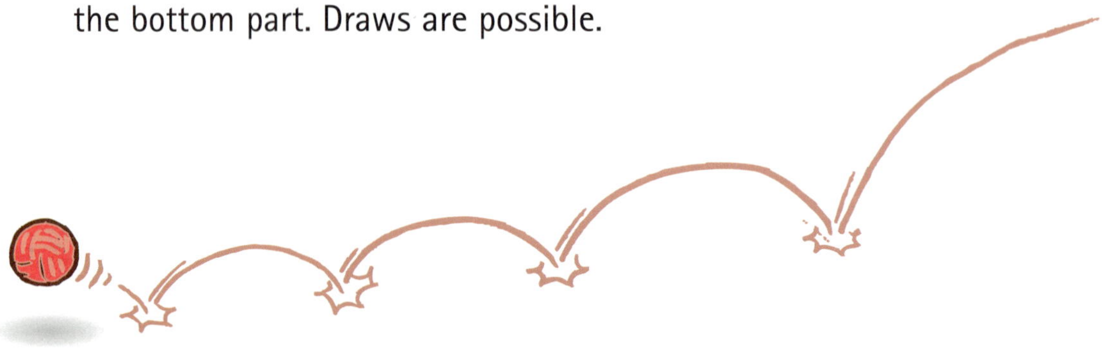

Chapter 7

Validation and VLookup

In this chapter and the next, you will build a spreadsheet which could be used in a post office or the mail room of a business. It will enable the post clerk to type in the weight and type of item being sent by surface mail and will then display the postage cost.

Planning the Spreadsheet

The first step is to get the raw data you wish to use in the model. For this system, the data could come from the Royal Mail website or from a booklet of postage rates obtainable at a post office.

The next step is to plan how the application will work, and hand-draw a sketch of what will appear on each sheet. This bit is often the hardest part!

We will be developing a simpler version for only one world zone and a small range of weights, but this could easily be developed into a full-blown application for a GCSE or AS Level project.

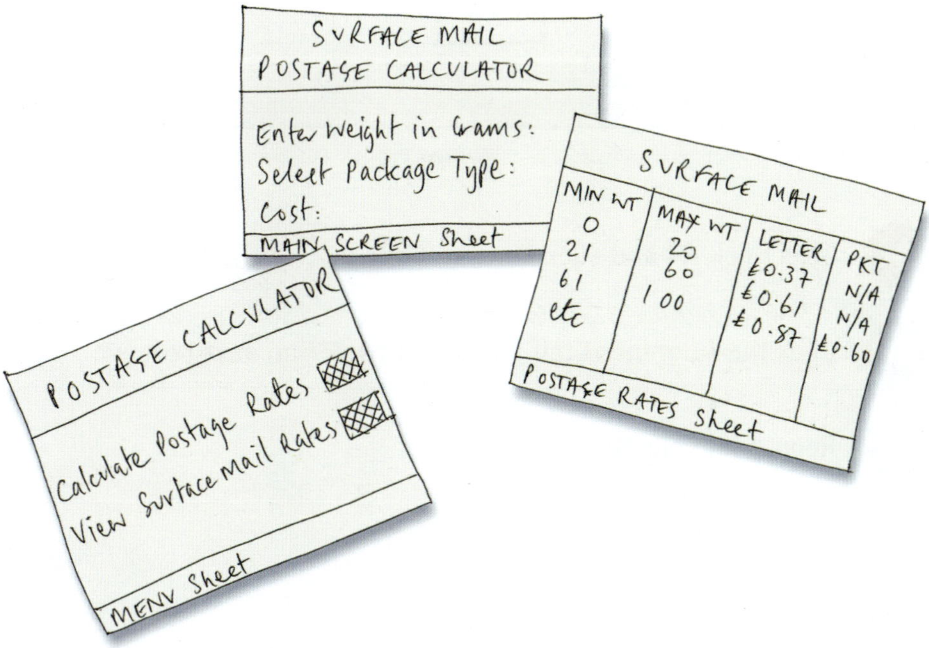

Building the Spreadsheet

Open a new workbook in Microsoft Excel.

Now you will enter the postage rates for letters in World Zone 1 and 2.

Type the heading Surface Mail in cell A1.

Centre the title across cell A1 to D1 using the Merge and Center button. Colour the cell Red, with White text, Bold, size 20.

Enter the rest of the data shown in Figure 7.1.

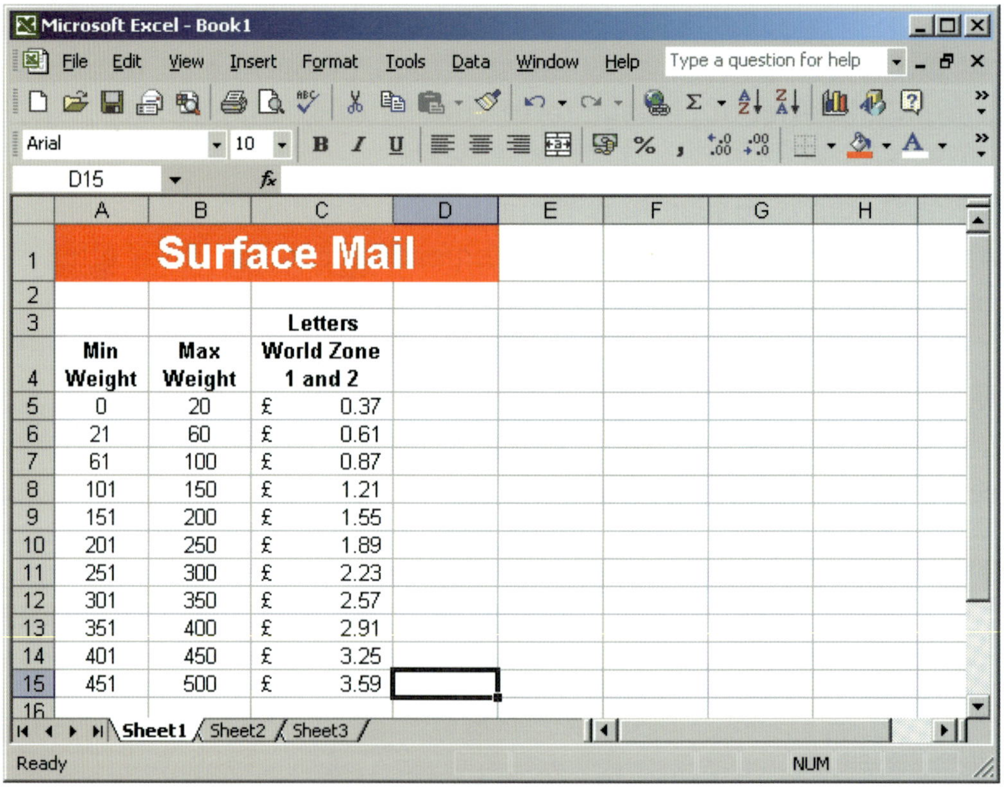

Figure 7.1

Select cell A4 and click Format, Cells...

Click the Alignment tab and check the Wrap Text box.

Repeat for cells B4 and C4.

Naming Ranges

You will have seen in Chapter 6 that an advantage of naming a range of cells is that it is much easier to understand references to it.

- Highlight cells A5 to C15.
- Select Insert, Name, Define... from the main menu.
- Name the selected range LetterPostage.

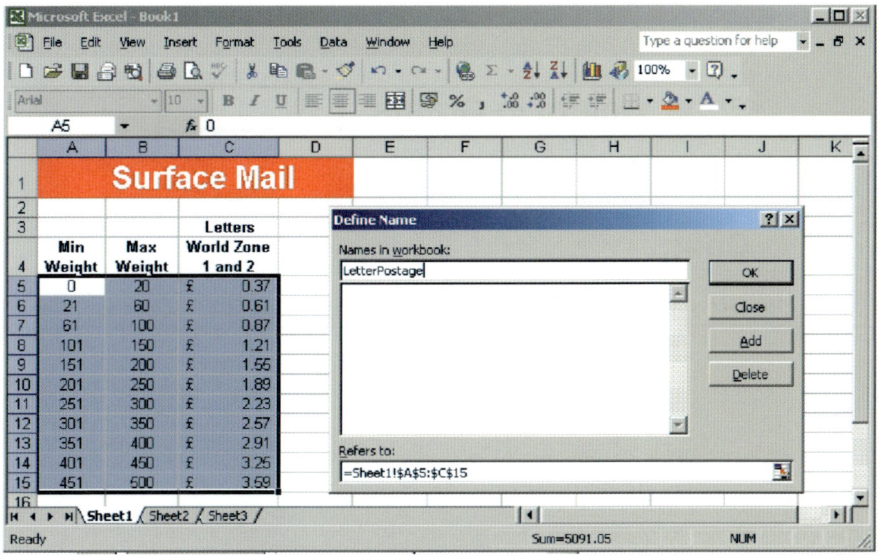

Figure 7.2: Naming a range of cells

- Click OK.

Moving and renaming sheets

We need a main screen into which the weight of the letter or packet will be entered.

- Drag the tab for Sheet 2 to the left of Sheet 1.
- Right-click the Sheet 2 tab and rename it MainScreen.
- Rename Sheet 1 PostageRates.
- Delete Sheet 3.

Designing the user screen

Now we can design the screen that the user will enter data into, and which will display the cost of posting the item.

- Click on the MainScreen tab.
- Copy the design as shown in Figure 7.3.

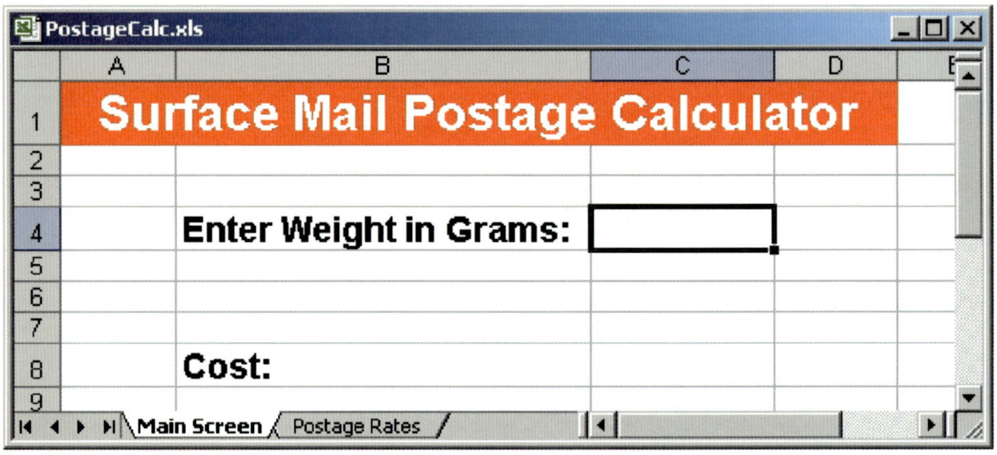

Figure 7.3: The front screen

- Save your work as PostageCalc.xls.

Adding validation to cells

Validation is the checking of input data by software, to make sure that it is sensible or reasonable.

In this case, validation is used to make sure that when the weight of the item is entered, it is within the allowed range. This reduces the chances of the user making an error when entering the weight.

- Click in cell C4.
- Select Data, Validation... from the menu.
- Select the options to allow a Whole number between 1 and 500 grams.
  (These are the smallest and largest weights in the table on the PostageRates sheet.)

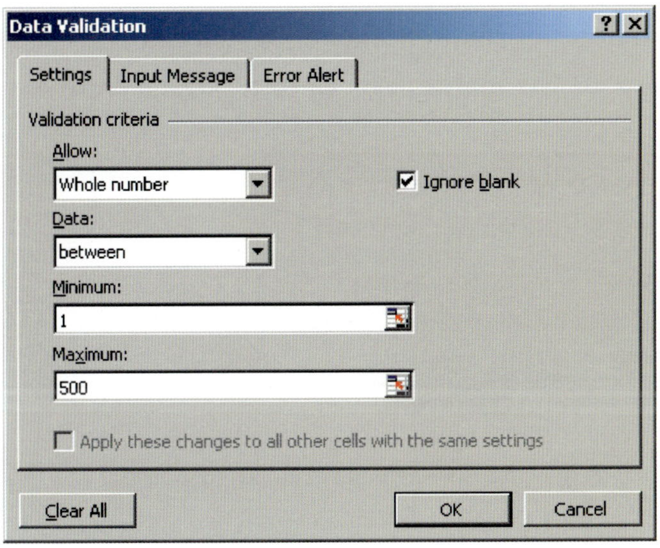

Figure 7.4: Adding validation to a cell

- Now click on the Input Message tab.
- Type Weight in the title box.
- Now type Please enter a weight between 1 and 500 grams.

Tip:
This is the message that will be displayed when someone clicks in cell C4.

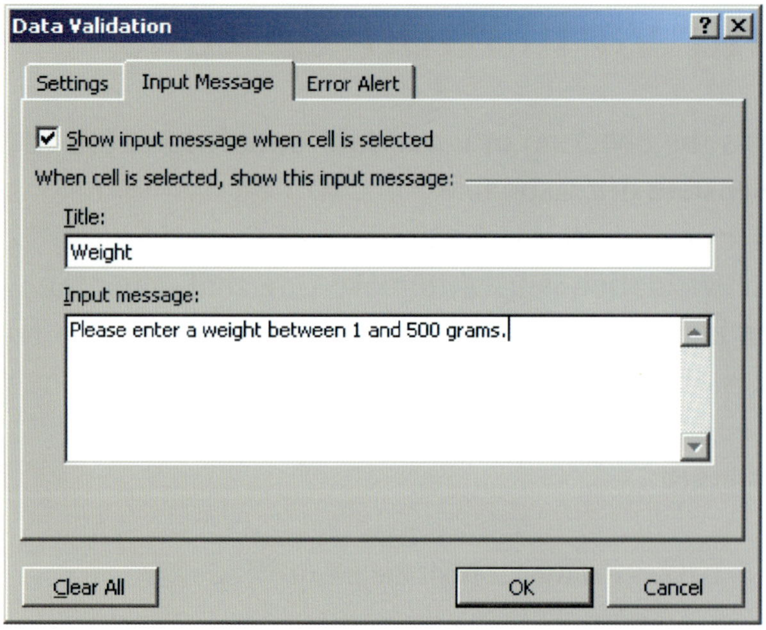

Figure 7.5: Entering an input message

- As a final touch, you can enter an error message to be displayed if a value outside your range is entered. Click on the **Error Alert** tab.
- Enter the text as shown in Figure 7.6. You can also change the style of the message box that appears when an invalid entry is made!

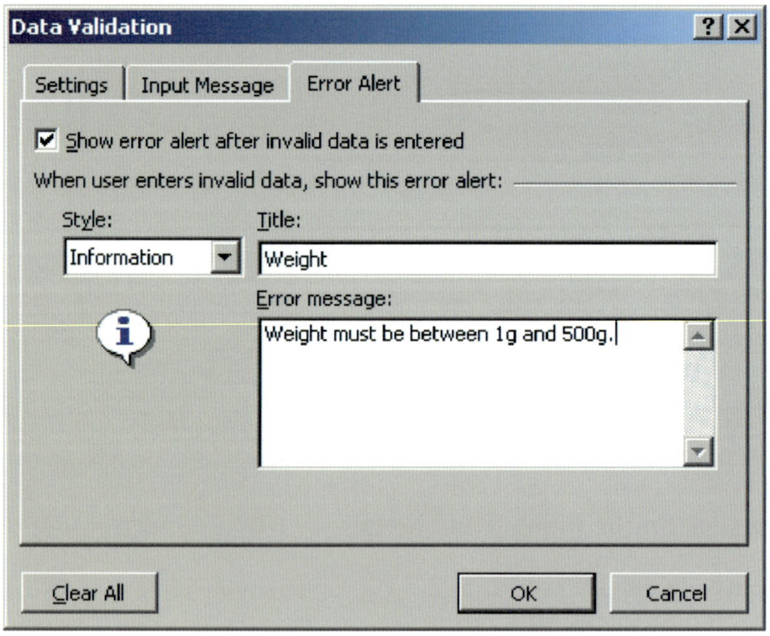

Figure 7.6: Adding an Error Alert

- Click **OK**.

Testing your validation

You should test that your validation rules work once you have made them. Try using extreme values that are just within your specified range and others just outside it.

- Click in cell C4. You will see your Input Message.
- Try entering 501. Press Enter.

Figure 7.7: Error!

- Now enter 20.

This value should be accepted.

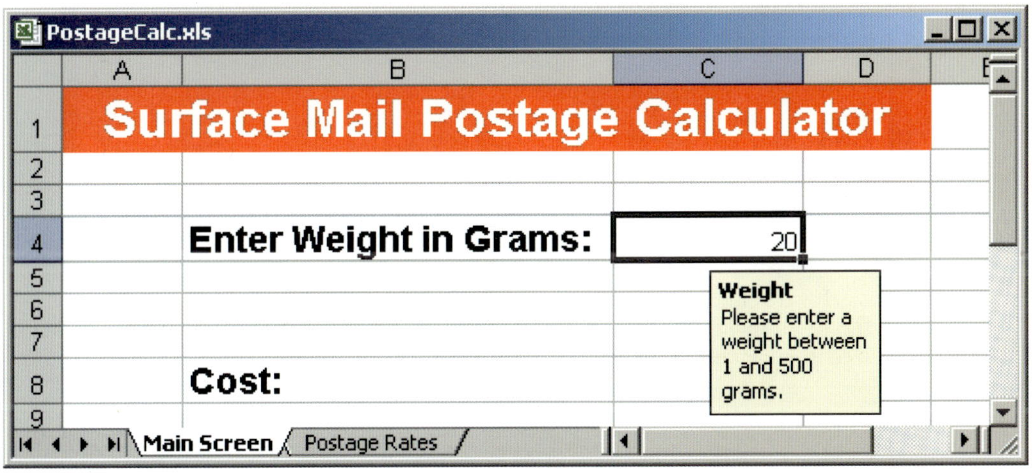

Figure 7.8

- Keep testing until you are sure your validation works correctly.
- Save your work.

The VLookup function

Now you need to make the correct postage price, relating to the weight you entered in C4, appear in C8. To do this you need the VLookup function.

- Select cell C8.

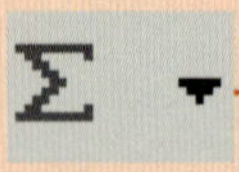

- Click the down arrow next to the AutoSum button. Select More Functions...
- Choose Lookup & Reference from the category list.
- Find VLOOKUP at the bottom of the function list. Click OK.

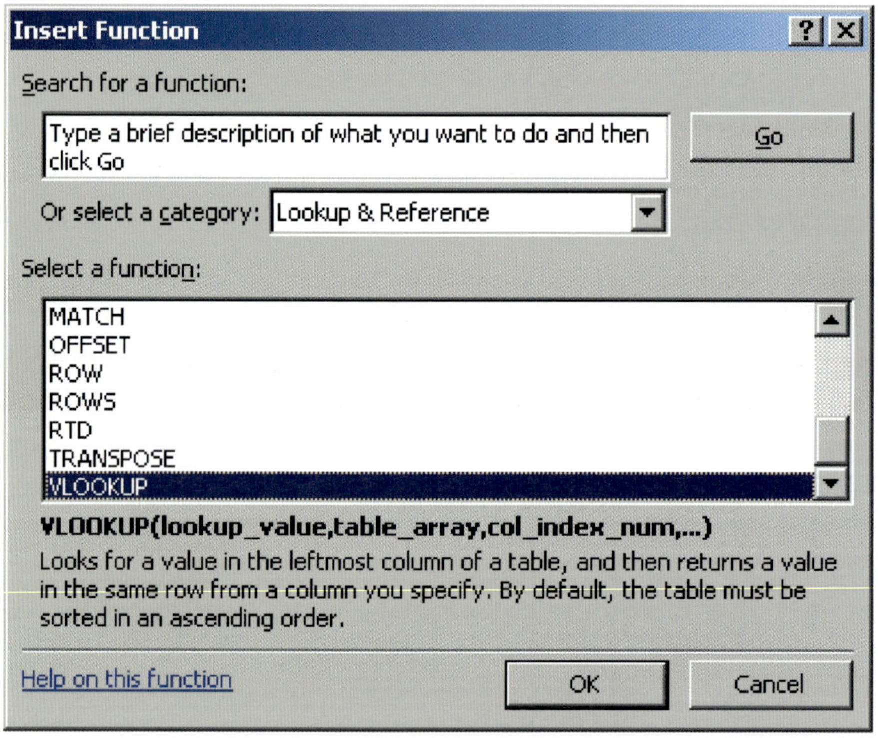

Figure 7.9: The VLookup function

- The Lookup_value is the cell value you want to find in a table. You need to enter C4 here.

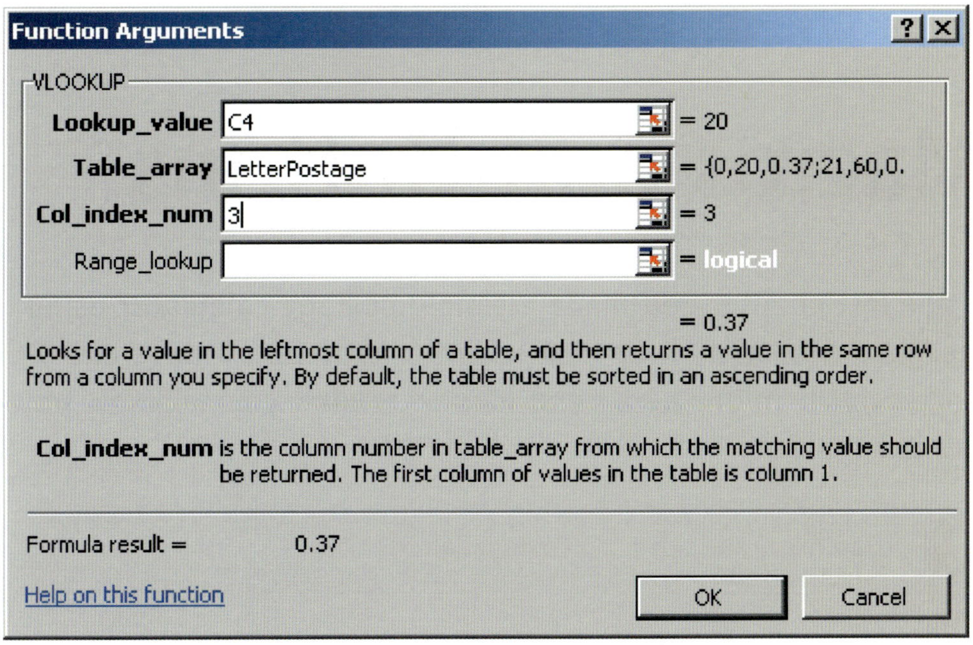

Figure 7.10: Using VLookup to find a cost

- Enter LetterPostage in the Table_array box. This is the range that contains all of the costs on the PostageRates sheet. (See Figure 7.1.)

VLOOKUP will look for the value that you enter in the first column of the table called LetterPostage. If it cannot find the exact value that you enter (for example, if you enter 73) it will default to the value below 73 and find the rate for a letter whose minimum weight is 61. That is the reason that we have used 2 columns for Minimum Weight and Maximum weight. There are other ways of doing this which you may be able to think of!

- Now you need to find the value in the third column of the LetterPostage table so enter a 3 in the Col_index_num box.

- Click OK.

- Try changing the weight of the letter in cell C4. What happens? How?

- Save your work and close Excel.

Tip:

VLookup will not work unless the Table_array you refer to is sorted in **Ascending** order.

Chapter 8 eight

Macros and Buttons

In the last chapter you made a simple postage calculator using the VLookup function to look up information on a different worksheet. It might be a good idea to remind yourself now how you did that!

- Load Excel and open the PostageCalc.xls file.
- Click on the PostageRates tab and put the cursor in cell D3.
- Enter the new column of data as shown below.

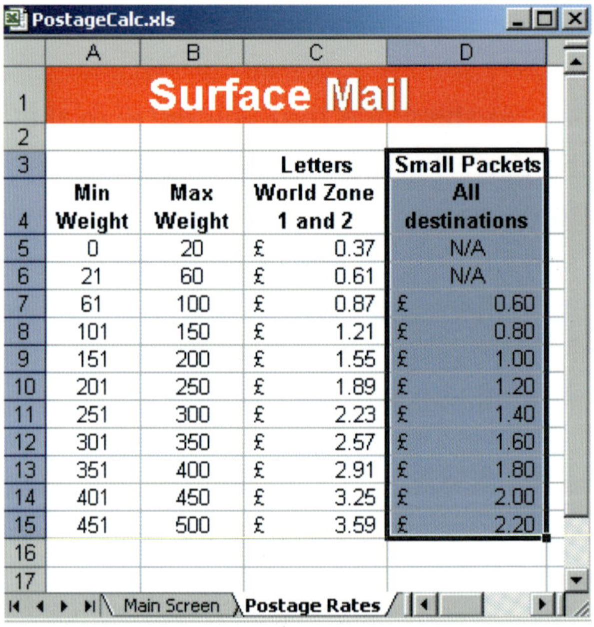

PostageCalc.xls

	A	B	C	D
1	Surface Mail			
2				
3			Letters	Small Packets
4	Min Weight	Max Weight	World Zone 1 and 2	All destinations
5	0	20	£ 0.37	N/A
6	21	60	£ 0.61	N/A
7	61	100	£ 0.87	£ 0.60
8	101	150	£ 1.21	£ 0.80
9	151	200	£ 1.55	£ 1.00
10	201	250	£ 1.89	£ 1.20
11	251	300	£ 2.23	£ 1.40
12	301	350	£ 2.57	£ 1.60
13	351	400	£ 2.91	£ 1.80
14	401	450	£ 3.25	£ 2.00
15	451	500	£ 3.59	£ 2.20
16				
17				

Main Screen | Postage Rates

Figure 8.1

Redefining a named range

The range called LetterPostage that you defined in Chapter 7 now needs to be redefined to include the costs for Small Packets in column D.

- Click Insert, Name, Define... on the main menu.
- Select LetterPostage.
- In the Refers to: box, click the Collapse Dialogue button and select cells A5 to D15.
- Press Enter.
- Click OK.

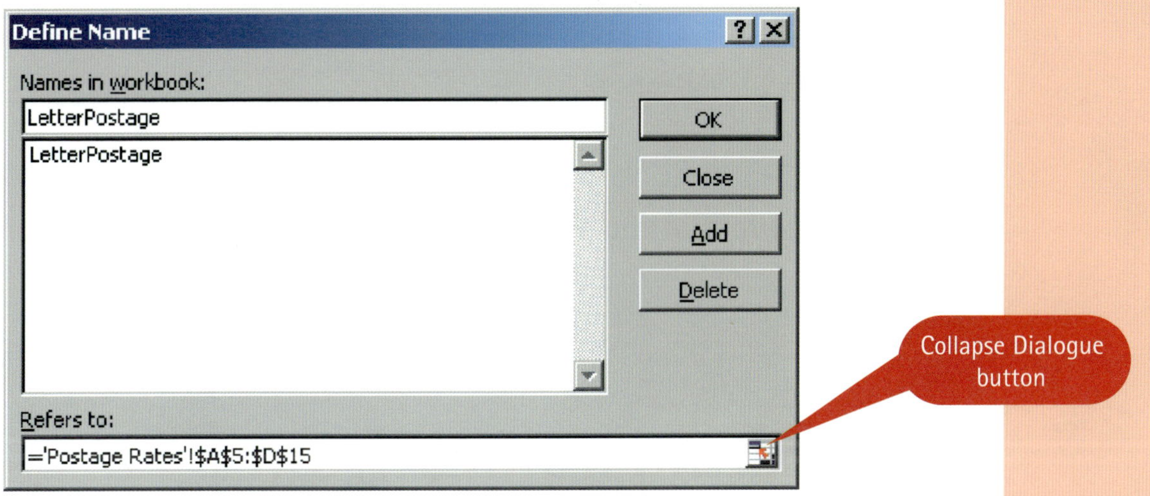

Figure 8.2: Redefining a named range

You now have an extra column of data to distinguish between Letters and Small Packets. Since these have different postage costs, you need a way of telling the spreadsheet which column you want it to read from, depending on what you are posting!

The Format Painter button

- Select the sheet called MainScreen.
- In cell B6, enter Select Package Type:.

- Select cell B4 and click the Format Painter button.
- Now click in cell B6.

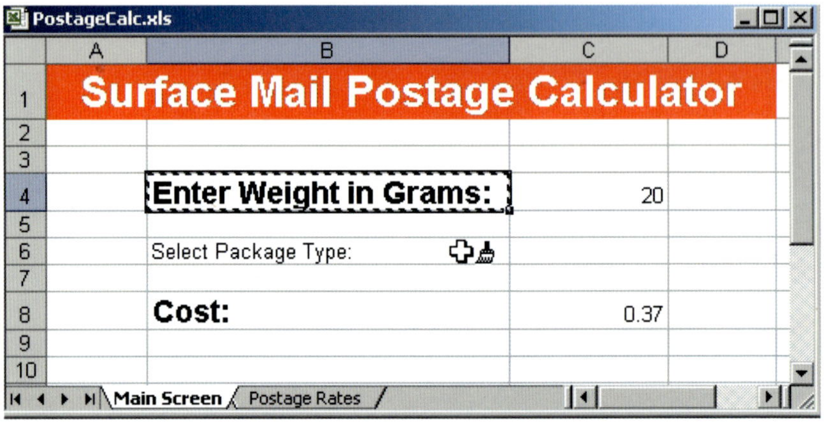

Figure 8.3: Using Format Painter

The same formatting as cell B4 will be applied to B6!

Selecting values from a drop-down list

In cell C6 you need to type either Letter or Small Packet in order to tell the spreadsheet which you are sending. It would be easy for a user to make a typing error, for example, typing Leter. The computer will not be able to interpret this and may return a wrong answer or an error message.

To prevent this happening, you can give the user a prewritten selection of valid options so that it is impossible to enter anything invalid.

Click in cell F2 and type Letter and in cell F3, type Small Packet.

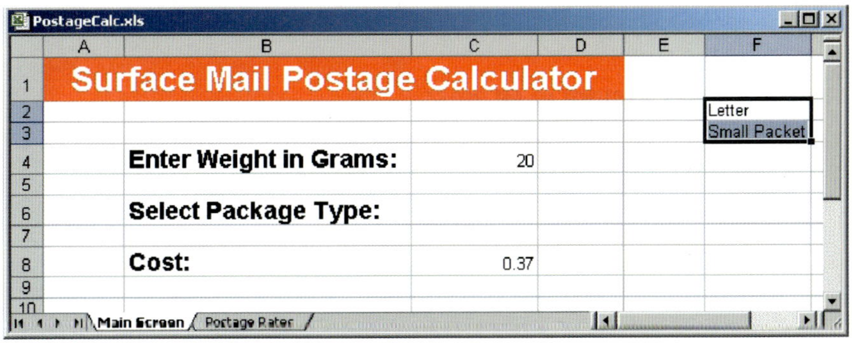

Figure 8.4

Now click in cell C6.

Select Data, Validation... from the menu.

On the Settings tab, choose List from the Allow: menu.

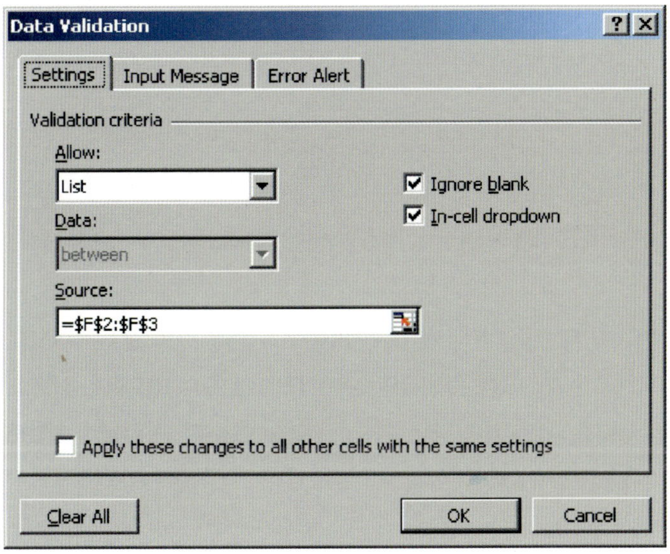

Figure 8.5: Validation

Tab to the Source: box and on the spreadsheet, highlight cells F2 to F3. Click OK.

Click on the small down-arrow next to cell C6 and see what appears!

Note:

This type of validation will only work if the list it refers to is on the same worksheet.

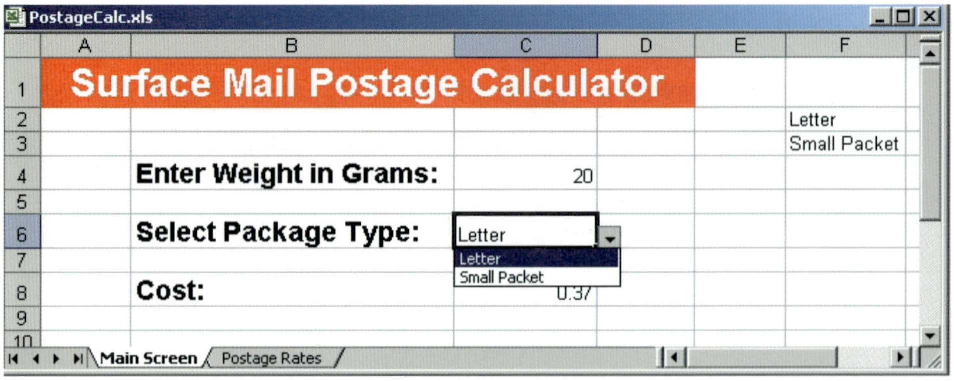

Figure 8.6

- You can Colour the Text in cells F2 and F3 White to hide them if you wish.

If.. Then.. Else.. & VLookup

Now we need to tell Excel what to do when either package type is selected. Try to understand the logic:

> **If..** *Letter* is selected, **Then..** look up the *Letter* cost, **Else..** look up the *Small packet* cost.

To do the looking up, we will need to use the VLookup function again, so in fact we are using one function inside another. To start off with, we will just do the If.. Then.. part. When that works we can add the Else.. part!

- Select cell C8. This formula needs to be amended like the example above.

- Click in the Formula Bar to edit the formula.

- Position the cursor just after the = at the beginning of the formula.

Type IF(C6="Letter", but DO NOT press Enter yet!

VLOOKUP =IF(C6="Letter",VLOOKUP(C4,LetterPostage,3)

Figure 8.7: Amending the formula

At the end of the formula add a closing bracket). Press Enter.

VLOOKUP =IF(C6="Letter",VLOOKUP(C4,LetterPostage,3))

Figure 8.8: The If.. Then.. part of the new formula

Test the new formula by choosing Letter as the Packet Type and changing the packet Weight.

It should work! Now you can add the last part of the formula to tell Excel what to do if *Small Packet* is selected as the package type.

Click in cell C8 and delete the last closing bracket). Type in a comma instead

Now add another VLOOKUP formula to find the cost for Small Packets.

Type in VLOOKUP(C4,LetterPostage, but DO NOT press Enter!

This time you will need to look in the fourth column of the LetterPostage table, so the last part of the VLOOKUP formula will be a 4 instead of a 3.

Enter 4 and two closing brackets)). One for the VLOOKUP and another to close the IF statement.

VLOOKUP =IF(C6="Letter",VLOOKUP(C4,LetterPostage,3),VLOOKUP(C4,LetterPostage,4))

Figure 8.9: Completing the IF statement

Make sure your formula is exactly the same as figure 8.9 and press Enter.

Test your new system!

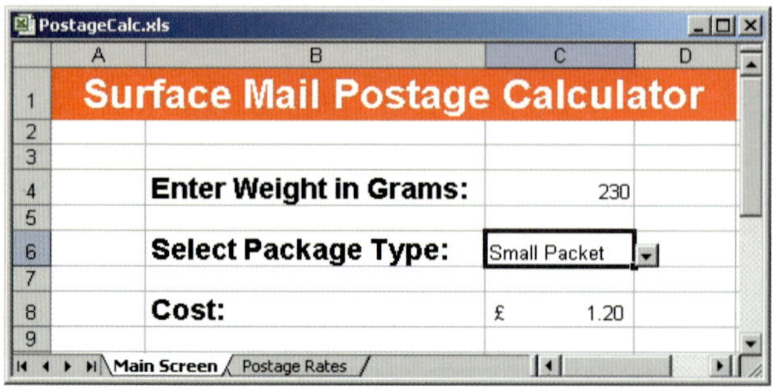

Figure 8.10

Save your work.

Tip:
Cell C8 should be formatted as currency.

Creating a menu screen

We need to create another new sheet which will display a menu of options. A menu screen would be even more important if you had included more comprehensive tables of postage rates for all zones of the world, surface mail and airmail, etc.

Right-click the sheet tab for MainScreen and insert a new worksheet.

Right-click the new tab and select Rename. Type in Menu and press Enter.

Right-click the tab again and select Tab Color...

Figure 8.11: Changing the tab colour

Change the colour to Red. Click OK.

Design a menu screen like the one in figure 8.12.

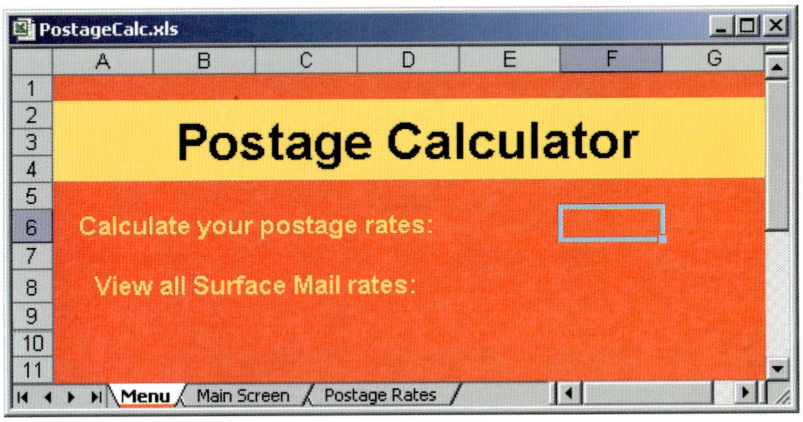

Figure 8.12: The menu screen

Adding ClipArt

From the Main Menu bar select Insert, Picture, ClipArt...

Select a suitable picture and move it into position on your menu screen.

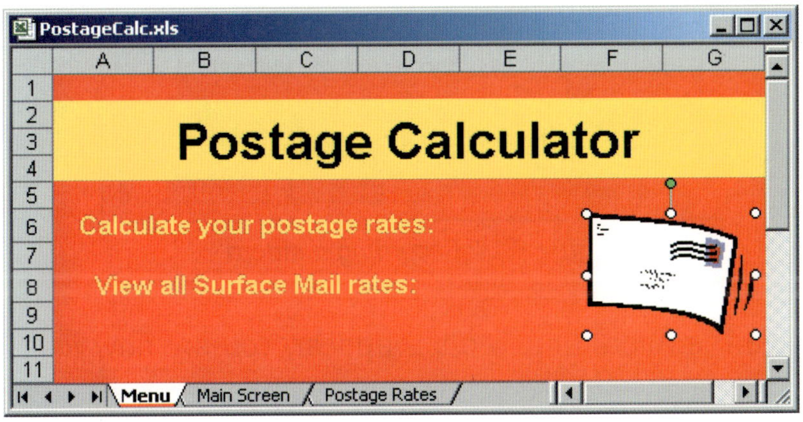

Figure 8.13: Adding ClipArt

Save your work.

Macros

A macro is a series of commands that is stored and grouped to run as a single command when you activate it by using a particular keystroke combination or by pressing a button.

For this project, a simple macro will be used to go to the MainScreen sheet from the Menu sheet and put the cursor in cell C4 ready to enter the letter or packet weight.

- Select the Menu worksheet.
- Click on Tools, Macro, Record New Macro...
- Call the macro MainScreen. Click OK.

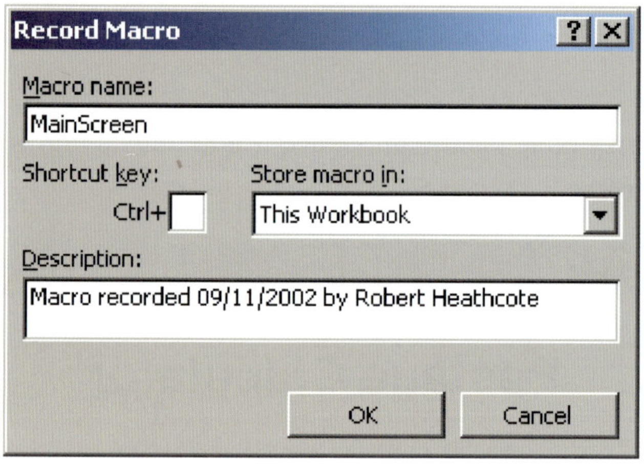

Figure 8.14: Recording a macro

You will see the Recording Toolbar appear. You are now in recording mode. Everything you do now will be recorded by Excel. Be careful here!

- Click on the MainScreen tab.
- Click in cell C4.
- Click the Stop Recording button. All done!

Figure 8.15

Buttons

Now you need to add a button which when pressed will run the macro.

- Select the Menu sheet tab.
- Click View, Toolbars, Forms from the menu.
- Select the Button tool.

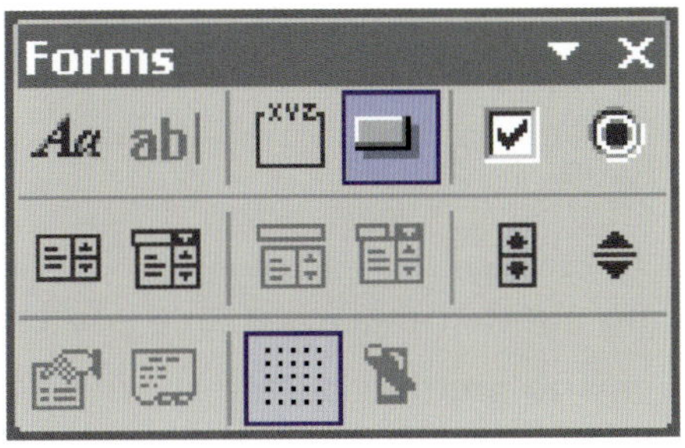

Figure 8.16

- Drag a small button onto your Menu screen, roughly over cells E6 to E7.
- The Assign Macro box will appear. Select the MainScreen macro and click OK.

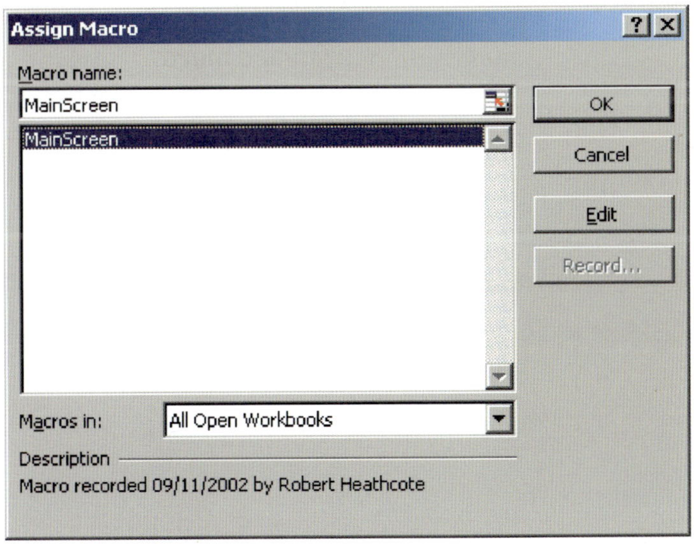

Figure 8.17: Assigning a macro to an object

Right-click the button and click Edit Text. Change the button text to Postage Calculator.

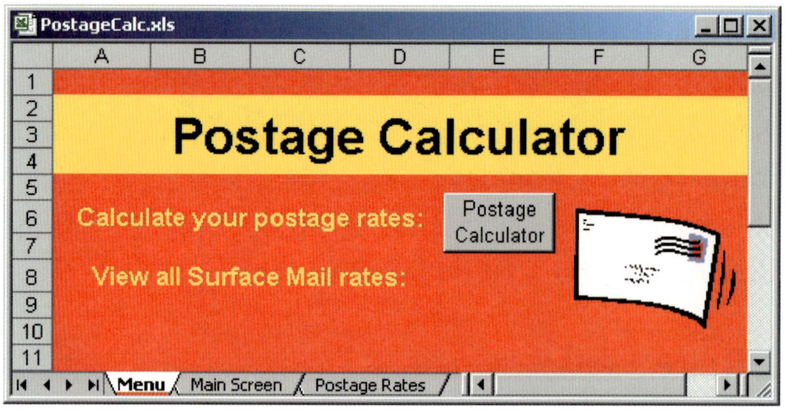

Figure 8.18

Test the new button!

Now try recording another macro to take you to the PostageRates sheet, and assign it to another button to View All Surface Mail Rates.

Protecting Cells

Now you can protect all the cells in your worksheet except the ones in which the user has to type data, i.e. C4 and C6 on the MainScreen sheet. Look back at Page 34 to remind yourself how to do this.

Save your workbook when you have finished. Now it's time to test it thoroughly.

Testing

If you are using Excel for project work, you will be required to show that you have tested your system thoroughly, that the spreadsheet works as expected and that you have not forgotten to include anything that the design specified. The application should not crash or give a wrong answer, whatever the user enters. Testing will involve three stages:

1. Draw up a test plan with test data to test every aspect of the application you have created. The test plan should specify the purpose of each test and what the expected result is. Test data should include extreme and invalid data.
2. Carry out each test and take a screenshot of the result, or print out the spreadsheet, to include in your documentation.
3. Correct any errors that appear and re-test until the expected result is achieved.

Here is part of a sample test plan:

Test	Purpose of test	Test data / method	Expected result
1	Make sure that the spreadsheet opens on the Menu sheet.	Open the spreadsheet.	Spreadsheet opens on the Menu sheet.
2	Test that user cannot change any of the formulae and labels in the spreadsheet.	Click in any cell except C4 and C6 and enter "abc".	Error message will appear to say that these cells are protected.
3	Test validation of Weight cell.	Enter "501" in cell C4.	Error message should warn that only values between 1 and 500 will be accepted.
4	Test extreme value of weight range.	Enter "500" in cell C4. Click "Letter" in cell C6.	Value should be accepted and the cost of Letter postage should be £3.59.
5	(etc)		
6			

Figure 8.19: Sample test plan

Presenting test results

As you carry out each test, take a screenshot of the result by pressing Alt and Prt Scr together. This copies an image of the screen into memory, from where it can be pasted into your Word document. You can crop the image to show just the part of the image that you want.

Annotate your test results by hand to highlight any points that are noteworthy.

Here is an example of test results:

Test 1 (Menu screen is displayed when spreadsheet is opened.)

The spreadsheet opened on the MainScreen sheet instead of the Menu screen. This was corrected by going to the Menu sheet and saving the file again. The test then performed correctly.

Test 2 (Showing that all cells except C4 and C6 are protected.)

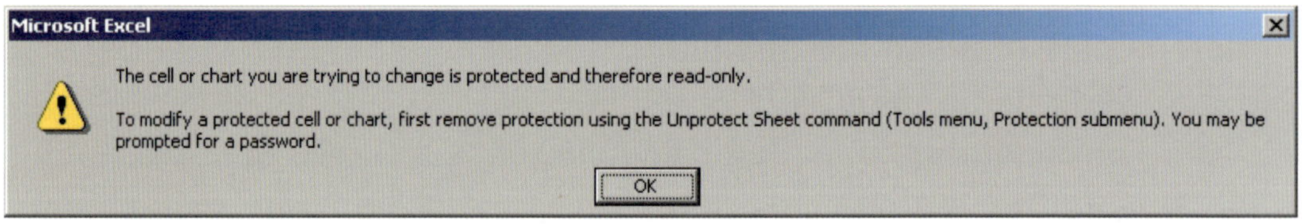

Initially the test did not work correctly as only the Menu sheet was protected. This was corrected by protecting each sheet individually.

Test 3 (Validation of weight cell.)

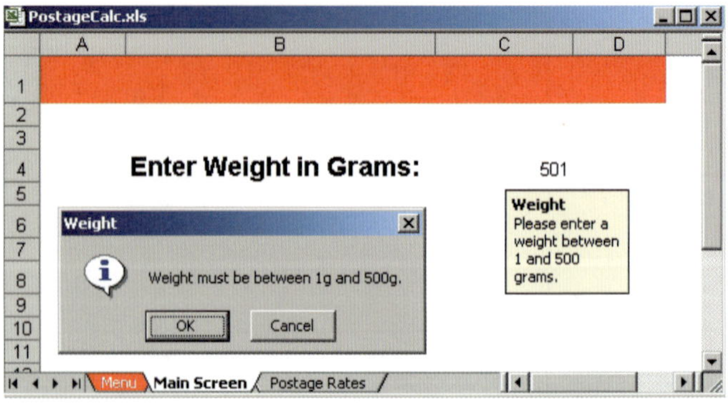

An error message was displayed when an invalid weight was entered.

Complete your test plan and results in a similar way!

Chapter 9

Charts

Charts and graphs are very useful to help interpret a set of figures. It is much easier to spot a trend or interesting fact from a bar chart, line graph or pie chart than by looking at a lot of numbers!

Suppose the local Sports Centre sells sweatshirts with a crest and name printed on them. They have been selling them for a year, and need to know how many to order for the next year. The manager wants to look at a graph of the monthly sales.

Entering the monthly sales figures

- Open a new worksheet and enter the heading Sweatshirt Sales 2002. Make it bold, size 16 and Merge and Centre the heading over cells A1 to C1. Widen the columns to accommodate the heading.
- Enter the other headings shown in Figure 9.1.
- Right-justify the headings in cells B3 and C3. Make the headings bold as shown.

	A	B	C	D
1	**Sweatshirt Sales 2002**			
2				
3	**Month**	**Unit Sales**	**Revenue**	
4	January			
5				

Figure 9.1: Starting the spreadsheet

- Save the worksheet as SalesChart.xls.

Using the Fill handle

Tip:
You can fill in the rest of the months without having to type them!

Click in cell A4, and drag the Fill handle in the bottom right hand corner downwards. Stop when the Tool tip says December and release the mouse button.

Entering a formula for revenue

The price of a sweatshirt is £12.00.

In cell A17 enter the heading Price of sweatshirt.

In cell C17 type 12 and press Enter. Format cell C17 as currency by pressing the Currency button.

In cell C4, enter the formula =B4*C17, but don't press Enter. Press the function key F4. This makes C17 an *absolute* value – you will see the formula in the formula bar change to =B4*$C$17. Now press Enter.

Enter monthly sales figures as shown.

	A	B	C	D
1	**Sweatshirt Sales 2002**			
2				
3	**Month**	**Unit Sales**	**Revenue**	
4	January	14	£ 168.00	
5	February	25		
6	March	32		
7	April	55		
8	May	47		
9	June	29		
10	July	16		
11	August	26		
12	September	67		
13	October	89		
14	November	52		
15	December	31		
16				
17	Price of Sweatshirt		£ 12.00	

Figure 9.2

Tip:
With all the revenues highlighted, Excel will tell you the sum of the cells in the bottom bar of the screen. It should equal £5796.00.

Use the Fill handle to copy the formula in cell C4 to cells C5 to C15.

Creating the chart

Now you can begin to build your chart. Since you have two different variables by month (**Unit Sales** and **Revenue**) you are going to make a custom chart with 2 vertical axes.

- Select all cells A3:C15.

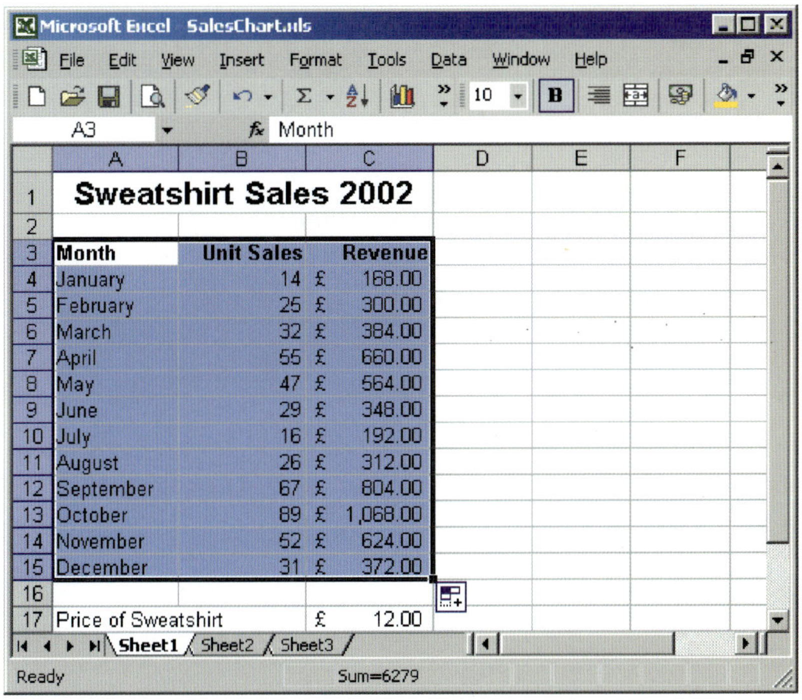

	A	B	C
1	Sweatshirt Sales 2002		
2			
3	Month	Unit Sales	Revenue
4	January	14	£ 168.00
5	February	25	£ 300.00
6	March	32	£ 384.00
7	April	55	£ 660.00
8	May	47	£ 564.00
9	June	29	£ 348.00
10	July	16	£ 192.00
11	August	26	£ 312.00
12	September	67	£ 804.00
13	October	89	£ 1,068.00
14	November	52	£ 624.00
15	December	31	£ 372.00
16			
17	Price of Sweatshirt		£ 12.00

Figure 9.3

- Click the **Chart Wizard** button.

- Click the **Custom Types** tab.
- Choose the **Line – Column on 2 Axes** chart and click **Next**.

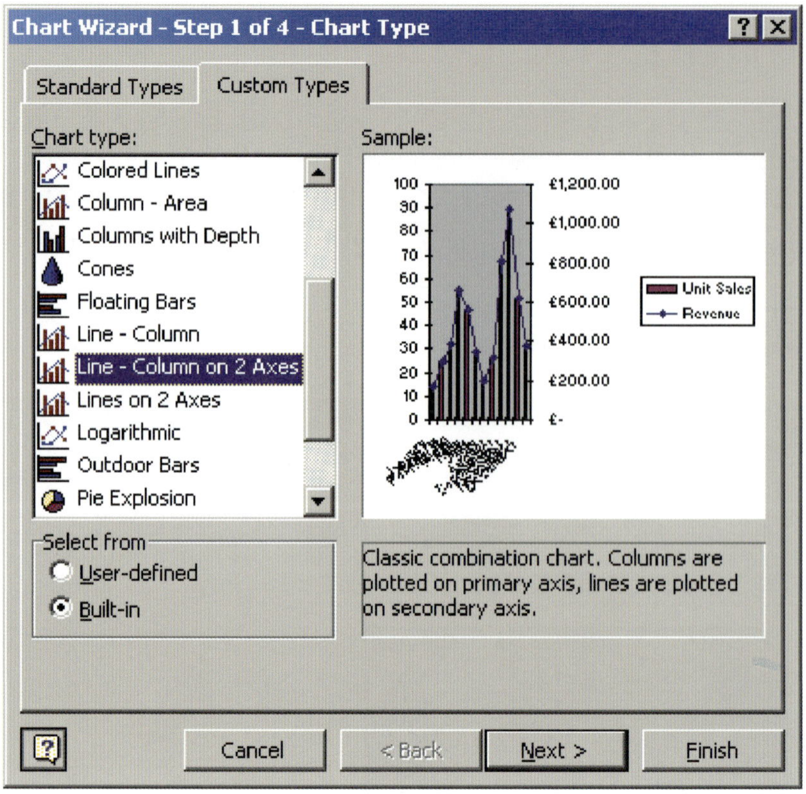

Figure 9.4: The Chart Wizard

- In the following screen, click **Next** again.
- Click the **Titles** tab and enter **Sweatshirt Sales 2002**.
- Enter the remaining titles shown in Figure 9.5.
- Click the **Legend** tab and select **Top**. Click **Next**.

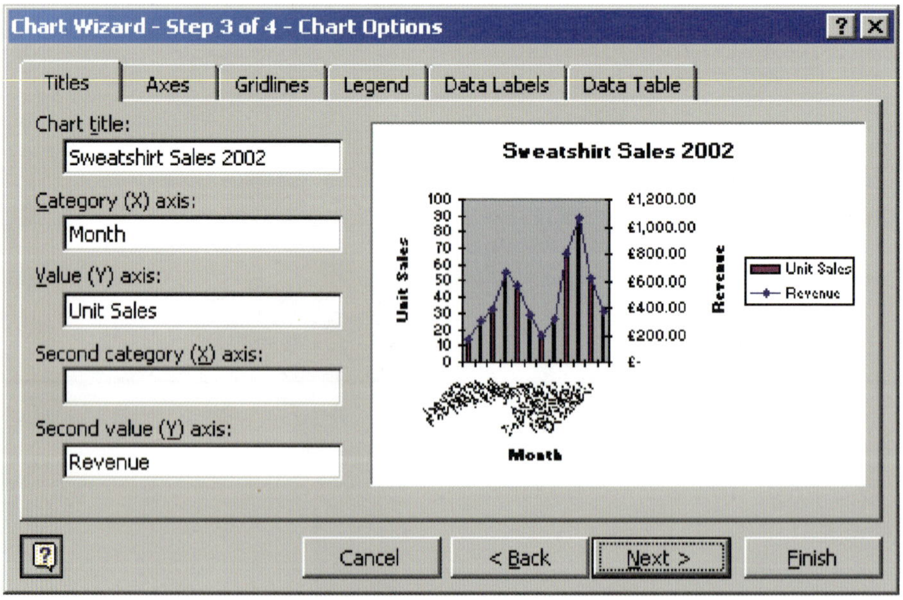

Figure 9.5: The Chart Wizard

Select the option to insert the chart As new sheet. Click Finish.

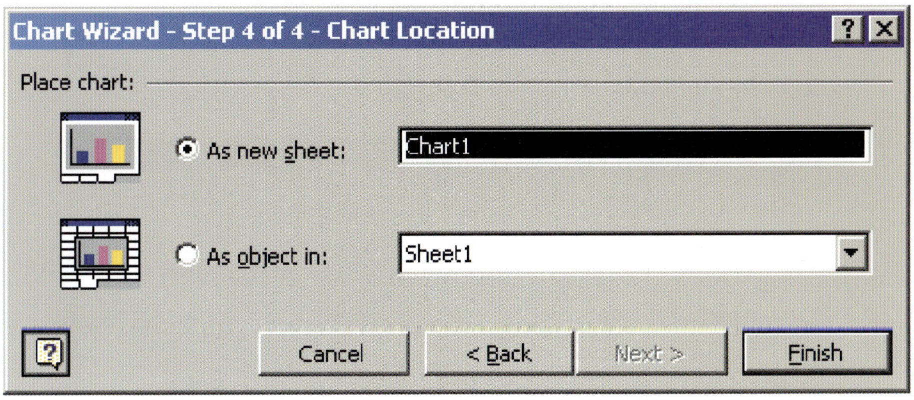

Figure 9.6: Inserting the chart into a workbook

Changing the chart scales

You will now see the chart appear on a new sheet called Chart1. To make it easier to distinguish between the unit sales and revenue trends you can change the scale of the unit sales bars.

Right-click the left Y axis.

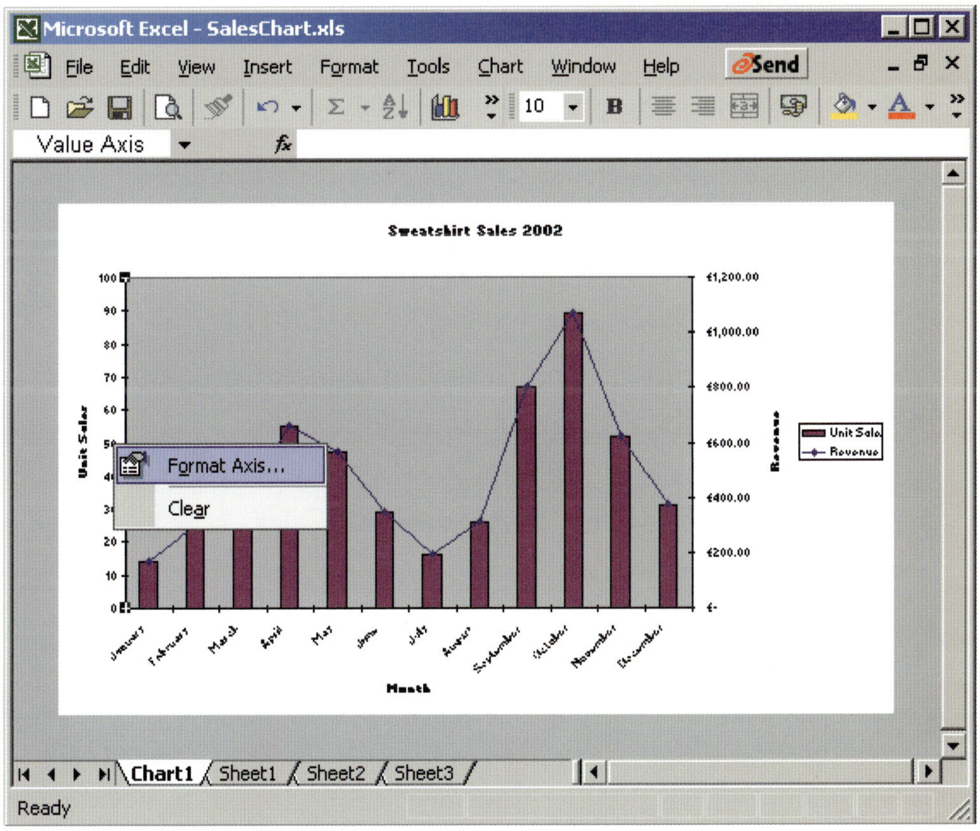

Figure 9.7: Formatting axes

- Click **Format Axis...**
- Click the **Scale** tab and change the **Maximum** to **150**. The other values should be as shown in Figure 8.8.

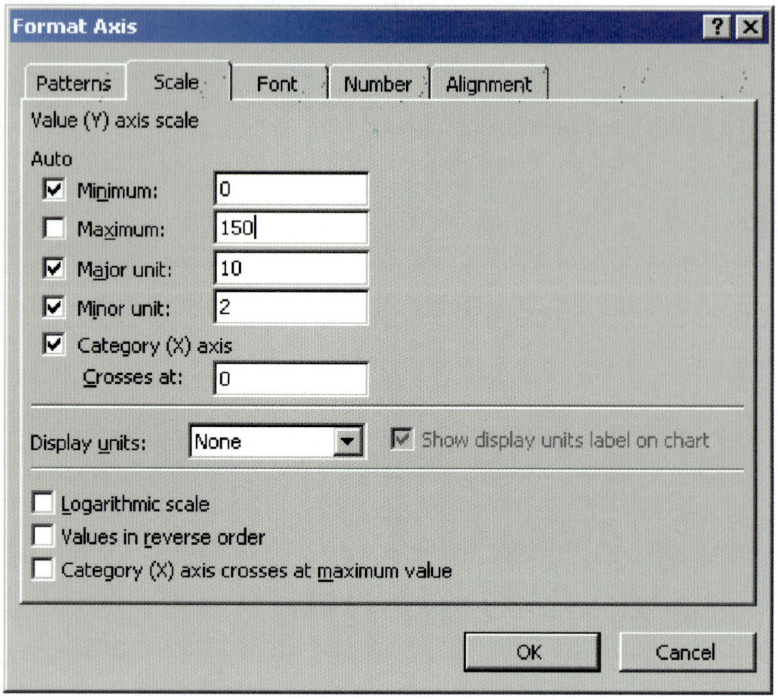

Figure 9.8: Changing the axis scale

- Click **OK**.
- Save your worksheet again (SalesChart.xls).

Adding Value Labels

It is sometimes difficult to read the exact value at a point in the graph so you can add value labels to make it easier.

- To display the point values of the revenue line right-click it.
- Select **Format Data Series...** from the pop-up menu.
- Click the **Data Labels** tab and select **Show Value**. Click **OK**.

Adding a Trendline

A trendline can be added to show the trend that figures are following. This is useful for making predictions as to what might happen next.

- Right-click a column in the Unit Sales series.
- Select **Add Trendline...** from the pop-up menu.
- With the **Type** tab selected, choose a **Linear** trend and the Unit Sales series.

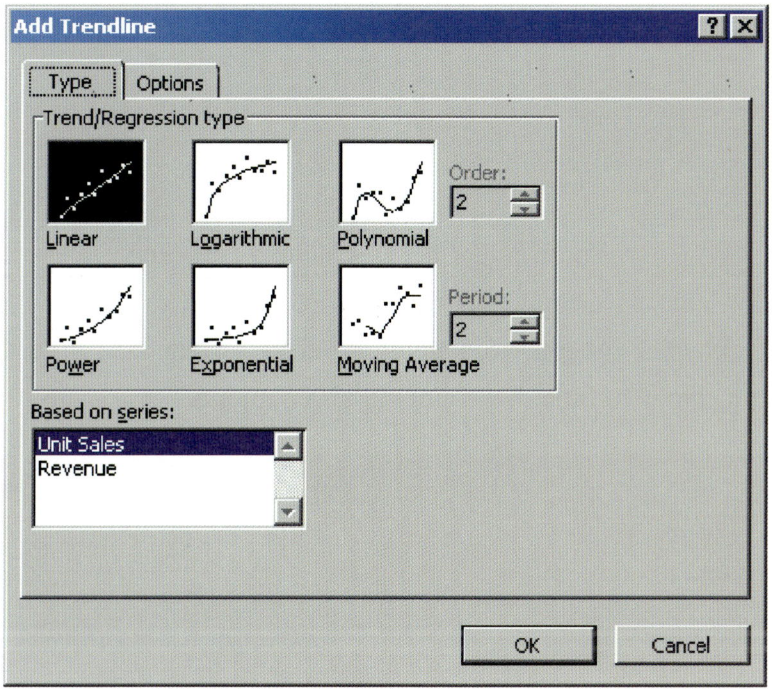

Figure 9.9: Adding a trendline

- Click **OK**.

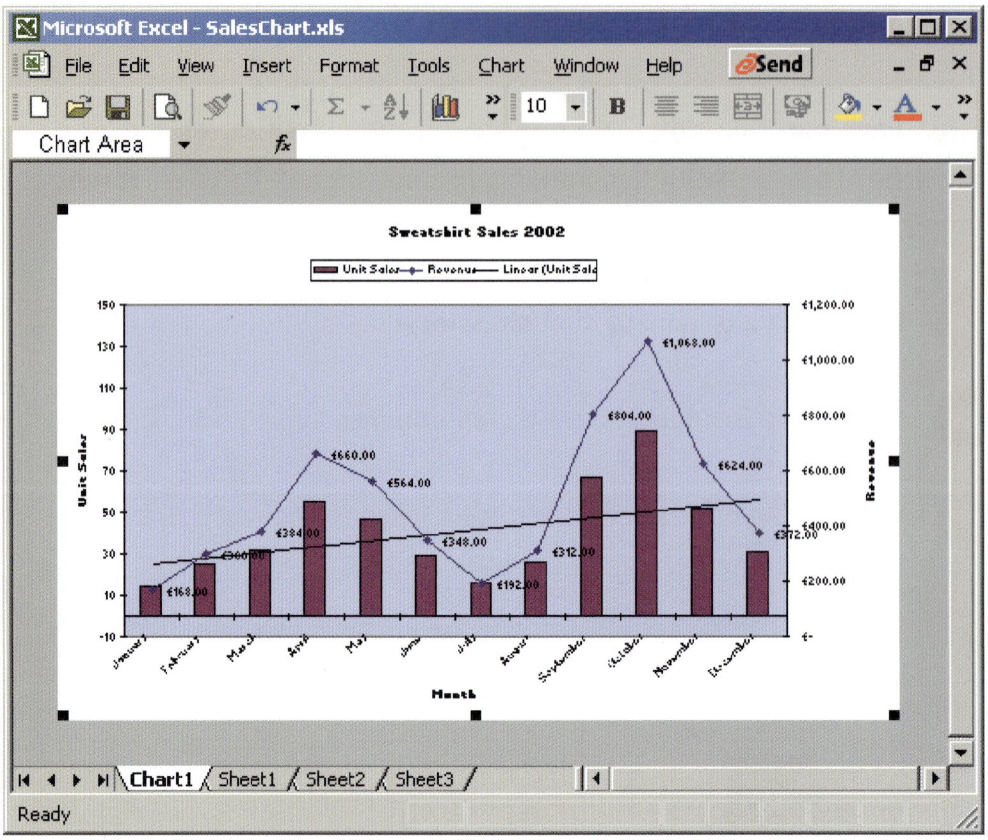

Figure 9.10: Chart with linear trendline

Right-click the grey plot area and select **Format Plot Area**. Change the colour to **Blue**. Try changing other colours.

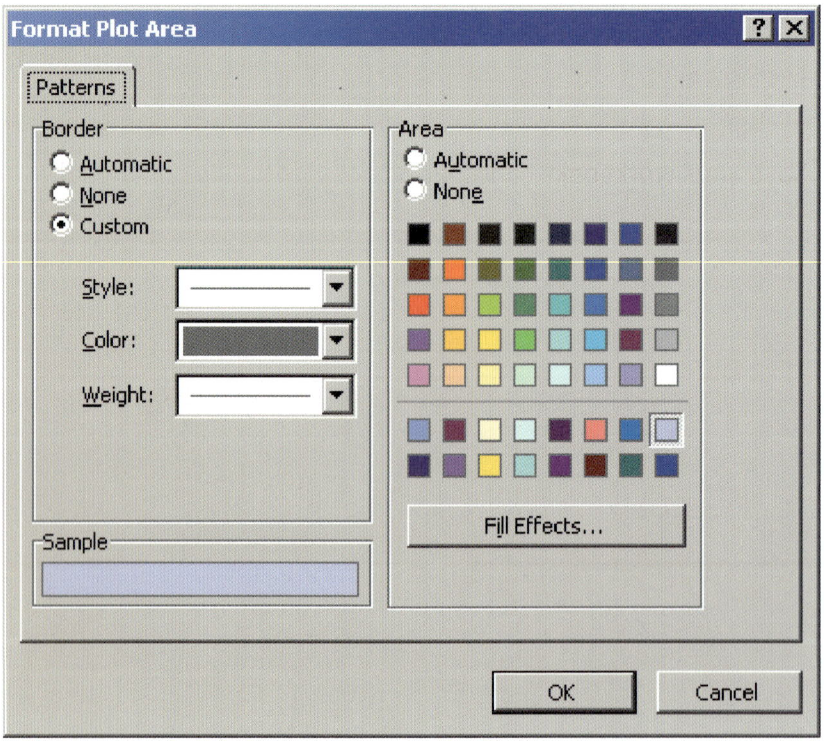

Figure: 9.11: The Format Plot Area window

Tip:

You can change the colour of any chart object by right-clicking it and selecting the **Format** option from the pop-up menu.

Adding a Header

- From the main menu select **View**, **Header and Footer...** Click the **Custom Header** button in the **Page Setup** window.

- In the **Header** window, enter your name in the **Left section**. Click in the **Middle section** and click the **Filename** button.

- Click in the **Right section** and click the **Date** button. Click **OK**.

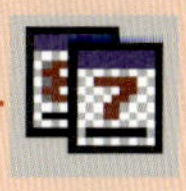

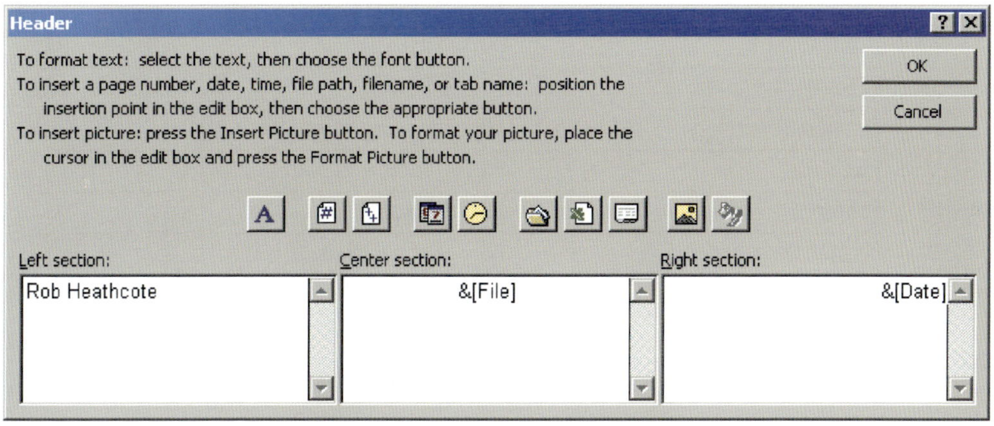

Figure 9.12: Adding a header

- Click **Print Preview** to see what the chart will look like when printed. Click the **Close** button in the Print Preview window to return to the chart.

- Save your workbook – another book successfully completed!

Index

Absolute reference 6, 13
Active cell 2
Alignment tab 38
Borders 40
Buttons
  Adding 67
  AutoSum 10
  Borders 16
  Chart Wizard 73
  Currency 8
  Date 20
  Fill 17
  Increase Decimal 12
  Merge and Center 3
  Paste Function 14, 30
Cell
  locking 34
  moving and deleting contents 4
Cell names
  deleting 44
  viewing 44
Chart Wizard button 73
Charts
  Adding Value Labels 76
  Changing scales 75
  Trendlines 77
Clip Art 31, 65
Column header 2
Copying formulae 5
Countif function 45
Create Names 43
Currency button 8
Data Labels 76
Date button 20
Deleting
  cell contents 4
  cell names 44
  sheets 51
Displaying formulae 21
Drop-down list 60
Entering formulae 5
Financial model 25
Fixed costs 25
Footer 19, 79
Format Data Series 76
Format Painter 60
Formatting
  negative numbers 17
  numbers 7
  text 8
  toolbar 2
Formula bar 2
Formulae
  entering and copying 5
  printing 22
Functions
  Countif 51
  IF 14
  If...then...else 30
  Sum 10
Header 19, 79
IF function 14, 62
Increase Decimal button 12
Locking cells 34
Macro 66
Menu screen 64
Merge and Centre 50
Modelling 25
Moving cell contents 4
Name Box 2, 29
Naming
  cell ranges 43, 51, 59
  cells 29
  sheets 51
Numbers, formatting 7
Page Setup 23
Paste Function button 14
Paste Special 37
Pointing 5
Printing formulae 22
Protecting your worksheet 34
Range names 45
Referencing cells
  Absolute 6
  Relative 6
Relative reference 6
Removing gridlines 32
Row header 2
Selecting non-adjacent cells 9
Set column width 3
Sheet tab 2
Sorting 47
Standard toolbar 2
Testing 69
Text
  formatting 8
  orientation 39
Toolbar
  Formatting 2
  Standard 2
Transpose 37
Trendline 77
Undo button 4
Unprotect Sheet 35
Validation 53, 60
Value Labels 76
Variable costs 25
Vertical alignment 38
VLookup 56
Wrap text 50